A TRAVEL GUIDE TO

Ancient
Alexandria

Other books in the Travel Guide series:

Ancient Athens
Ancient Rome
California Gold Country
Renaissance Florence
Shakespeare's London

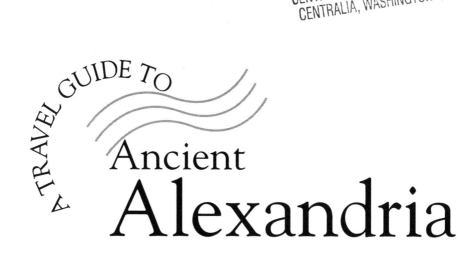

A TRAVEL GUIDE TO

Ancient
Alexandria

Don Nardo

**LUCENT
BOOKS®**

THOMSON
™
GALE

San Diego • Detroit • New York • San Francisco • Cleveland • New Haven, Conn. • Waterville, Maine • London • Munich

THOMSON
━━━━✦━━━━ ™
GALE

© 2003 by Lucent Books. Lucent Books is an imprint of The Gale Group, Inc., a division of Thomson Learning, Inc.

Lucent Books® and Thomson Learning™ are trademarks used herein under license.

For more information, contact
Lucent Books
27500 Drake Rd.
Farmington Hills, MI 48331-3535
Or you can visit our Internet site at http://www.gale.com

LIBRARY OF CONGRESS CATALOGING-IN-PUBLICATION DATA

Nardo, Don, 1947–
   Ancient Alexandria / by Don Nardo.
      p. cm. — (The travel guide to:)
Summary: A historical look at ancient Alexandria and its people, education, weather, transportation, hotels, shopping, festivals, sporting events, banks, government, and sightseeing.
Includes bibliographical references (p.) and index.
   ISBN 1-59018-142-5 (hardback : alk. paper)
   1. Alexandria (Egypt)—Civilization—Juvenile literature. 2. Alexandria (Egypt)—Description and travel—Juvenile literature. [1. Alexandria (Egypt)—Civilization.] I, Title. II. Series.
   DT73 .A4 N37 2003
   962'.1—dc21

                                                 2002006599

Printed in the United States of America

Contents

Travel can be a unique way to learn about oneself and other cultures. The esteemed American writer and historian, John Hope Franklin, poetically expressed his conviction in the value of travel by urging, "We must go beyond textbooks, go out into the bypaths and untrodden depths of the wilderness and travel and explore and tell the world the glories of our journey." The message communicated by this eloquent entreaty is clear: The value of travel is to temper one's imagination about a place and its people with reality, and instead of thinking how things may be, to be able to experience them as they really are.

Franklin's voice is not alone in his summons for students to "travel and explore." He is joined by a stentorian chorus of thinkers that includes former president John F. Kennedy, who established the Peace Corps to facilitate cross-cultural understandings between Americans and citizens of other lands. Ideas about the benefits of travel do not spring only from contemporary times. The ancient Greek historian Herodotus journeyed to foreign lands for the purpose of immersing himself in unfamiliar cultural traditions. In this way, he believed, he might gain a firsthand understanding of people and ways of life in other places.

The joys, insights, and satisfaction that travelers derive from their journeys are not limited to cultural understanding. Travel has the added value of enhancing the traveler's inner self by expanding his or her range of experiences. Writer Paul Tournier concurs that, "The real meaning of travel, like that of a conversation by the fireside, is the discovery of oneself through contact with other people."

The Lucent Books' Travel Guide series enlivens history by introducing a new and innovative style and format. Each volume in the series presents the history of a preeminent historical travel destination written in the casual style and format of a travel guide. Whether providing a tour of fifth-century B.C. Athens, Renaissance Florence, or Shakespeare's London, each book describes a city or area at its cultural peak and orients readers to only those places and activities that are known to have existed at that time.

A high level of authenticity is achieved in the Travel Guide series. Each book is written in the present tense and addresses the reader as a prospective foreign traveler. The sense of authenticity is further achieved, whenever possible, by the inclusion of descriptive quotations by contemporary writers who knew the place; information on fascinating historical sites; and travel tips meant to explain unusual cultural idiosyncrasies that give depth and texture to all great cultural centers. Even shopping details, such as where to buy an ermine, trimmed gown or a much-needed house slave, are included to inform readers of what items were sought after throughout history.

Looked at collectively, this series presents an appealing presentation of many of the cultural and social highlights of Western civilization. The collection also provides a framework for discussion about the larger historical currents that dominated not only each travel destination but countries and entire continents as well. Each book is customized by the author to bring to the fore the most important and most interesting characteristics that define each title. High standards of scholarship are assured in the series by the generous peppering of relevant quotes and extensive bibliographies. These tools provide readers a scholastic standard for their own research as well as a guide to direct them to other books, periodicals, and websites that will provide them greater breadth and detail.

A Note to the Reader

I n this volume, various aspects of the history, society, and culture of the ancient city of Alexandria are examined in the format of a modern travel guide. This unusual approach provides an innovative and entertaining way to learn about ancient Greek, Roman, and Egyptian life and ideas. At the same time, however, it presents some technical problems that do not exist in straightforward history texts.

The most obvious of these problems is that a number of accepted conventions of dating, measurement, and so forth have changed over the centuries. Today, for example, most history books automatically use B.C., meaning "before Christ," and A.D., denoting the Christian era. In the standard B.C.-A.D. scheme, the date for Alexandria's founding, an event described in this volume, is 331 B.C., or 331 years before the beginning of the Christian era.

The difficulty is that the B.C.-A.D. dating system did not exist in ancient times; Christian scholars introduced it in the early Middle Ages. The people of the ancient Mediterranean world had a number of different dating systems of their own, which often existed side by side. It stands to reason, therefore, that if this travel guide had actually been written in ancient times, the author would have used one of the dating systems then accepted. However, using such an obscure and unfamiliar system in a modern book would not be very practical; so for the sake of clarity and convenience, this book uses the standard B.C.-A.D. dating system.

Another concern is the dating of the travel guide itself. The author has chosen the year A.D. 160 for a number of reasons. First, by that time Alexandria had been in existence for almost five hundred years and had passed from

Greek rule to Roman domination. And the city's local ethnic groups—native Egyptians, Greeks, Jews, Romans, and others—had become firmly established and had interacted for several centuries. This time setting allows the reader to better appreciate the city's cosmopolitan nature. Also, by the year in question, Alexandria's most important and famous monuments and institutions had been created; the city's university, the ancient world's main center of learning, had produced its greatest minds; and the city had reached its height of commercial prosperity. All of these factors strongly encouraged tourism. And as the second most important city in the Mediterranean world—after Rome—Alexandria was an immensely popular tourist spot, attracting visitors from across that world and beyond.

Just as the peoples of the Mediterranean world had their own dating systems, they had their own units of measurement. But as in the case of dates, this book employs modern units of measurement—miles and square miles—as well as degrees of temperature and so forth, to make the text more understandable to modern readers. Except for these conventions, all aspects of this travel guide are authentic. They are based on evidence derived from surviving ancient literary texts and studies made by archaeologists and other scholars of paintings, sculptures, buildings, tools, weapons, coins, and other ancient artifacts. All of the places and sites described were real. And the ruins of a few of these sites still exist in modern Alexandria, now one of the world's oldest and still one of its greatest cities.

CHAPTER ONE

A Brief History of Alexandria

Alexandria is truly one of the greatest cities in the known world. In fact, only Rome, the seat of power of the empire that rules that world, can lay claim to more political and commercial importance. Part of Alexandria's success derives from its location. It is nestled in the western sector of Egypt's Nile Delta, on a narrow strip of land separating Lake Mareotis and the Mediterranean Sea. From that vantage, it oversees the outflow of Egypt's grain and other material riches to ports near and far; it also stands at a strategic crossroads between the Mediterranean's western cities and cultures and those of the Near East, of which Egypt is a part.

Yet Alexandria's position in Egypt is somewhat deceiving. First-time visitors to the city are often surprised to find that it bears little resemblance to other Egyptian towns. Some of its inhabitants are native Egyptians, to be sure. But most are Greek, and Greek remains the city's dominant tongue, though its rulers are Roman and large numbers of Jews, Syrians, and other peoples reside here. Indeed, Alexandria's founder intended it to be the most cosmopolitan city in the world. And today, in the year A.D. 160, nearly five hundred years since he initiated its planning, it still lives up to that vision.

Connecting Egypt to the Greater World

That founder, of course, was Alexander III, the Macedonian Greek king who has come to be called "the Great." In 334 B.C., he led his army into Asia and began his rapid conquest of the mighty Persian Empire, centered near the

Persian Gulf. After defeating the Persian king at Issus, in northern Syria, Alexander made his way down the eastern Mediterranean coast, besieging and capturing city after city.

Finally, Alexander reached Egypt, which had been under Persian domination for many years. The Egyptians welcomed him as a liberator. And he entered their ancient capital of Memphis in triumph. Memphis did not seem to him to be ideal as a capital, however, for it lay some ninety miles from the sea, and he was far-sighted enough to realize that Egypt's ultimate usefulness and success would rest on a viable connection to the greater Mediterranean world.

So Alexander determined that he would build a new capital for Egypt in the Nile Delta. According to the most popular version of the event, he remembered a passage from the *Odyssey*, one of the great epic poems by the esteemed Greek bard Homer; in it, Homer mentions "an island called Pharos in the rolling seas off the mouth of the Nile,"[1] said to be ideal for sailors launching ships northward into the sea. According to Alexander's Greek biographer, Plutarch of Chaeronea, Alexander

immediately visited Pharos. At that time it was still an island near the

This is only a small section of Alexandria, widely viewed as the second-most splendid and important city in the known world next to Rome itself.

11

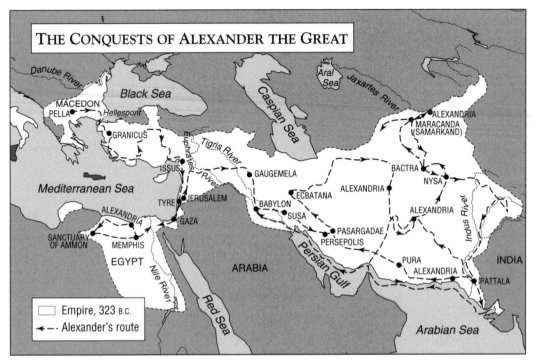

THE CONQUESTS OF ALEXANDER THE GREAT

Danube River

Black Sea

Aral Sea

Jaxartes River

Caspian Sea

MACEDON
PELLA
Hellespont

ALEXANDRIA
MARACANDA
(SAMARKAND)

GRANICUS

Tigris River

Euphrates River

BACTRA

NYSA

ISSUS

Mediterranean Sea

GAUGEMELA

ALEXANDRIA

TYRE JERUSALEM

ECBATANA

BABYLON

ALEXANDRIA

Indus River

ALEXANDRIA

GAZA

SUSA

SANCTUARY
OF AMMON

MEMPHIS

PASARGADAE

PERSEPOLIS

EGYPT

Nile River

ARABIA

Persian Gulf

PURA

ALEXANDRIA

INDIA

Red Sea

PATTALA

☐ Empire, 323 B.C.
◄ – · Alexander's route

Arabian Sea

Canopic mouth of the Nile, but since then it has been joined to the mainland by a causeway. When he saw what wonderful natural advantages the place possessed—for it was a strip of land resembling a broad isthmus which stretched between the sea and a great lagoon [Lake Mareotis], with a spacious harbor at the end of it—he declared that Homer, besides his other admirable qualities, was also a far-seeing architect, and he ordered the plan of the city to be designed so that it would conform to this site.[2]

The architect in charge of planning the new city was Deinocrates, of the Greek island city-state of Rhodes. But various historians who have chronicled Alexander's deeds all agree that the king himself personally designed the city's general layout. While he was doing so, an omen, or sign of future events, occurred, one that foreshadowed the city's multicultural development. "There was no chalk to mark the ground plan," Plutarch wrote.

So they took barley meal, sprinkled it on the dark earth, and marked out a semi-circle, which was divided into equal segments by lines radiating from the inner arc to the circumference. The shape was similar to that of a *chlamys*, or military cloak, so that the lines proceeded, as it were, from the skirt, and narrowed the breadth of the area uniformly. While the king was enjoying the symmetry of the design, suddenly huge flocks of birds appeared from the river and the lagoon, descended upon the site, and devoured every grain of the barley. Alexander was greatly disturbed by this omen, but the diviners [those in charge of interpreting omens] urged him to take heart and interpreted the occurrence as a sign that the city would not only have abundant resources of its own, but would be the nurse of men of innumerable nations, and so he ordered those in charge of the work to proceed.[3]

The Ptolemaic Dynasty

As it turned out, Alexander never saw a single building rise on the site of the great city named for him. Not long after liberating Egypt, the king headed eastward to fulfill his destiny—the complete conquest of Persia. After a whirlwind campaign that took him as far as India, he returned to one of the former Persian capitals, Babylon, and died there in 323 B.C. His leading generals and governors then began warring among themselves, each

An Island in the Highways of the Fish

Greek sailors knew about the Pharos Island, future home of the great city of Alexandria, Egypt, many centuries before either the Greeks or Romans gained widespread control of the Mediterranean sea lanes. Proof lies in this excerpt from Homer's great epic poem, the Odyssey *(quoted here from E.V. Rieu's translation). On his way home from the Trojan War, Menelaus, king of the Greek city of Sparta, was blown off course and landed in Egypt. Describing his stay there, Menelaus recalls:*

There is an island called Pharos in the rolling seas off the mouth of the Nile, a day's sail out for a well-found vessel with a roaring wind astern. In this island is a sheltered cove where sailors come to draw their water from a well and can launch their boats on an even keel into the deep sea. It was here that the gods kept me idle for twenty days; and all that time there was never a sign on the water of the steady breeze that ships require for a cruise across the open sea. . . . [Luckily, a goddess appeared and said:] "Sir, I will tell you all you need to know. This island is the haunt of that immortal seer, Proteus of Egypt, the Old Man of the Sea, who owes allegiance to [the Greek sea god] Poseidon and knows the sea in all its depths. He is my father too. . . . If you could contrive somehow to set a trap and catch him, he would tell you about your journey and the distances to be covered, and direct you home along the highways of the fish.

Alexander (crouching right) shows his design for Alexandria's layout to his chief architect, Deinocrates. Alexander selected the Nile Delta as the ideal location for the city because of its accessibility to the Mediterranean world.

hoping to secure for himself as much of Alexander's enormous empire as possible.

The power struggle in Egypt was relatively short-lived. Alexander had left an associate, Cleomenes, in charge of the country. A greedy, corrupt individual, Cleomenes proceeded to tax the people heavily and to extort money from local priests and other high-placed Egyptians. But one of Alexander's strongest, most capable generals—Ptolemy (TAW-luh-mee)—soon put a stop to this. Reaching Egypt with a loyal band of troops, Ptolemy immediately put Cleomenes to death.

Making sure that Deinocrates had all the necessary resources to continue constructing the new capital of Alexandria, Ptolemy then went about the business of establishing a permanent power base. First, he seized the body of Alexander, which was on its way westward from Persia. He placed the corpse in a coffin of gold in a magnificent tomb—the Soma—in Alexandria. Possession of the great conqueror's remains gave Ptolemy a strong appearance of legitimacy and credibility as Alexander's natural successor. At first, Ptolemy ruled Egypt in the dead man's name. But in time, he declared himself king and also took the title of Soter, or "Savior." In this way, Ptolemy established a new ruling family—the Ptolemaic dynasty—which remained in power for three centuries.

The City's Greek Privileged Class

By the time that Ptolemy I Soter died, in the 280s B.C., he had come to rule an empire that included Palestine, the large island of Cyprus, and parts of Asia Minor,[4] as well as Egypt itself. Two other major new Greek kingdoms had recently emerged nearby.

One was the Seleucid Kingdom, established by Alexander's follower Seleucus; it encompassed the lands north and west of the Persian Gulf— the heart of the old Persian Empire— and parts of Asia Minor. The other was the Macedonian (or Antigonid) Kingdom, created by Antigonus Gonatas (grandson of another of Alexander's associates, Antigonus the One-Eyed); the Antigonid realm was made up mostly of Macedonia and portions of the Greek mainland. These great kingdoms competed with Ptolemaic Egypt for control of the

Alexander's leading generals pay their last respects to him in Babylon. He died soon afterward and Ptolemy seized his body and brought it to Alexandria.

15

The Founding of Alexandria

The first and greatest biographer of Alexander the Great was the Greek historian Arrian, who was born in the late first century A.D. In this excerpt from his Anabasis Alexandri, *Arrian tells about the establishment of the city of Alexandria in 331 B.C.*

From Memphis he sailed down the river again with his guards and archers . . . to Canopus, when he proceeded round Lake Mareotis and finally came ashore at the spot where Alexandria, the city which bears his name, now stands. He was at once struck by the excellence of the site, and convinced that if a city were built upon it, it would prosper. Such was his enthusiasm that he could not wait to begin the work; he himself designed the general layout of the new town, indicating the position of the market square, the number of temples to be built, and what gods they should serve—the gods of Greece and the Egyptian Isis— and the precise limits of its outer defenses. He offered sacrifice for a blessing on the work; and the sacrifice proved favorable.

lands, peoples, and trade routes of the Near East and eastern Mediterranean.

From their still growing capital of Alexandria, the Ptolemies ruled Egypt as it had always been ruled, as a monarchy. For the average Egyptian, apart from the fact that the royal family was now Greek, nothing had really changed. Meanwhile, increasing numbers of Greeks migrated to Alexandria. Sanctioned and encouraged by the country's Greek rulers, Greek merchants, soldiers, and administrators were able to establish a privileged class in the capital, as well as in many other parts of Egypt. Greek became the universal language of administration and business, and those who could not speak, read, and write it found it difficult, if not impossible, to get ahead in life. In general, the status of native Egyptians, as well as Jews

and other ethnic residents, was inferior to that of Greeks in the marketplace, the army ranks, and society as a whole.

Meanwhile, the Ptolemies established magnificent structures and institutions in Alexandria, making it a showcase for all humanity. Each of these rulers added to the local palace complex until it had no rival in size and splendor in the known world. Adjoining this complex were the Museum, a university where scholars from many lands congregated (and still congregate) to study and experiment, and the Great Library, where the Ptolemies collected the works of all the known authors. Perhaps most famous and imposing of all, the Ptolemies erected the Pharos, a towering lighthouse, on the island of the same name. They also constructed a causeway joining the island to the mainland portion of the city.

Cleopatra, Caesar, and Antony

The Ptolemies fulfilled Alexander's dream of opening up Egypt to world trade and culture. And in the process, they made Alexandria one of the most popular tourist attractions in the world. Yet these monarchs were ultimately unable to maintain control of the magnificent city and empire they had created. First, after the reign of the first three Ptolemies, their successors grew increasingly ineffective and unpopular as rulers. They often overtaxed the people, and they maintained a cultural barrier between the Egyptian masses and the royal court, where Greek language and ways were supreme. To the disdain of many natives, none of the Ptolemies, except for the last, even bothered to learn the Egyptian tongue.

This last Ptolemy was, next to the first, the greatest of the line. She was Cleopatra VII, daughter of Ptolemy XII Auletes. By the time of her birth, in 69 B.C., Rome had already conquered the Macedonian and Seleucid realms, and Egypt, though still independent, had become a third-rate power. Indeed, on the international scene, Rome, now the most powerful nation-state in the world, dominated Egypt, which had become its client (a state economically and militarily dependent to another).

During a power struggle with her younger brother, Ptolemy XIII, the young Cleopatra was banished from the royal palace in Alexandria. But then she shrewdly enlisted the aid of one of the leading Romans of the day, Julius Caesar, who was visiting the city at the time. Caesar was very taken with the intelligent and ambitious young woman, and they became lovers. An eminently practical man, Caesar realized that, as his lover and confidant, Cleopatra would make him and Rome a valuable ally. So

The astronomer Hipparchus measures the latitude of a planet from a terrace at the Museum.

Cleopatra Rules Alexandria

Cleopatra, last of the Ptolemies, proved to be one of the better rulers of the dynasty. Proof of her wise administrative policies and concern for her people's welfare takes the form of a surviving decree [quoted in Jack Lindsay's Cleopatra] issued in her name from Alexandria on April 13, 41 B.C.:

Nobody should demand of them [the farmers] anything above the essential Royal Dues [basic taxes], [or] attempt to act wrongfully and to include them among those of whom rural and provincial dues, which are not their concern, are exacted [collected]. We, being extremely indignant [about overtaxation] and considering it well to issue a General and Universal Ordinance [regulation] regarding the whole matter, have decreed that all those from the City [Alexandria], who carry on agricultural work in the country, shall not be subjected, as others are, to demands for *stephanoi* and *epigraphai* [gifts and special taxes people were forced to give the government] such as may be made from time to time. . . . Nor shall any new tax be required of them. But when they have once paid the essential Dues, in kind [in the form of goods and services] or in cash, for cornland and for vineland . . . they shall not be molested for anything further, on any pretext whatever. Let it be done accordingly, and this [decree] put up in public, according to Law.

he reinstalled her on the Egyptian throne with great pomp and ceremony.

Eventually, Caesar returned to more pressing duties abroad. He departed Alexandria early in 47 B.C., leaving Cleopatra in control of the city and country. Three years later, he was assassinated in the Roman Senate. But it was not long before Cleopatra had a new Roman benefactor—Marcus Antonius,[5] one of Caesar's closest supporters. Antony was even more captivated by Cleopatra than Caesar had been.

The lovers eventually became embroiled in a Roman civil war against Antony's rival, Octavian, who was also Caesar's adopted son. If Cleopatra and Antony had won, they would have made Alexandria the capital of a new empire embracing both the West and East. At the time, this would probably have been quite fitting; the city had become widely known for its openness to ideas and customs from diverse lands and peoples. However, the lovers lost their bold bid for world power. The war was decided by a single battle, fought at Actium, in western Greece, in 31 B.C. After their defeat, Cleopatra and Antony returned to Alexandria. And there, as Octavian closed in on them, they committed suicide.

Alexandrian Hospitality

The victorious Octavian took personal charge of Alexandria and Egypt. A rather austere individual, he disliked the city's diversity and the openness and independent, pleasure-loving spirit of its people. Also, the Alexandrians were not particularly happy about having a Roman from across the sea impose his will on them, and they gave him a cold reception. So Octavian built a town nearby for himself, calling it Nicopolis, or "City of Victory." To him, Alexandria remained little more than a conveniently located port from which to ship Egyptian grain back to Italy to feed and thereby control the hungry masses.

Alexandria's proud inhabitants were no less insolent to Octavian's successors. Three years after the death of Cleopatra, the Roman senate conferred on him the name of Augustus, "the revered one," and he became the first of the fifteen emperors who have since ruled the Roman Empire, including Egypt and its capital. When one or another of these rulers visited the city, the Alexandrians would praise him to his face. But behind his back they

Octavian visits the tomb of Alexander during his first trip to Alexandria. The Greek and Egyptian natives gave him a cool reception, as they did most of his successors.

Death of a Proud Queen

One of the more dramatic and romantic episodes in Alexandrian history was the death of Cleopatra. Legend has it that she allowed herself to be bitten by an asp, a poisonous snake, rather than do the bidding of her Roman opponent, Octavian. Learning of the proud Egyptian queen's intended suicide, Octavian ordered some men to stop her. But they were too late. "When they opened the doors," Plutarch writes in his biography of Antony [in Makers of Rome*],*

they found Cleopatra lying dead upon a golden couch dressed in her royal robes. Of her two women [maid-servants], Iras lay dying at her feet, while Charmian, already tottering and scarcely able to hold up her head, was arranging the crown which encircled her mistress's brow. Then one of the guards cried out angrily, "Charmian, is this well done?" And she answered, "It is well done, and fitting for a princess descended of so many royal kings," and, as she uttered the words, she fell dead by the side of the couch.

would ridicule him. Hadrian, who ruled the empire from A.D. 117 to 138, declared that the people of the city "are seditious, vain, and spiteful—though as a body [they are] wealthy and prosperous."[6]

Presently, Antoninus Pius is emperor. He has proven to be a fair and judicious ruler and has therefore gained favor among many Alexandrians, including some of those who have long opposed all Roman leaders. The last serious anti-Roman disturbance in the city was a full seven years ago (A.D. 153), when a small mob rioted and killed the governor.[7]

It must be emphasized that such violent acts happen infrequently and are almost always directed at authority figures. The people of Alexandria are inherently friendly and regularly welcome ordinary visitors from all lands, including Italy. This attitude often comes as a surprise. Many travelers arrive expecting to meet real versions of stereotypical Alexandrians—selfish, self-absorbed people interested only in making money and indulging in frivolous luxury. In reality, the proportion of people fitting this description is no greater in Alexandria than in other cities. Most Alexandrians are not only hospitable, but also refreshingly honest, independent, and self-reliant. They remain fiercely proud of their unique heritage and splendid urban monuments, and invite travelers to witness these wonders firsthand.

CHAPTER TWO

Weather and Physical Setting

Visitors almost always find Alexandria's climate ideal and its setting beautiful and impressive. Dealing with the climate first, the city features a modified version of what is often termed "Mediterranean" weather, characterized by long, hot, dry summers and relatively short, cool winters. The average temperature in the high season of July and August is about 86° F. By contrast, in the winter months—November, December, and January—the temperature dips to an average of 64° and only very rarely goes below 50°.

Winter is also the rainy season. Almost all of the roughly ten inches (250 mm) of rain that falls on Alexandria each year comes between November and February. By any standards, this is a very modest volume of rain. Moreover, almost no rain at all falls in the summer months.

Even to the casual observer, therefore, it becomes immediately apparent that the city does not receive the rainfall necessary to sustain a large urban population for very long. Luckily, Alexander's architect, Deinocrates, and subsequent Ptolemaic engineers worked out a solution to this problem. Namely, they installed a marvelous system of cisterns throughout the city. These underground tunnels and vaults are constructed of stone and designed to store large amounts of water for long periods. The system of cisterns is connected to a canal that runs for twelve miles (20 km) to the Nile's Canopic branch. Luckily, the Nile gently floods during the summer months. So, unlike the inhabitants of so many other lands, at the height of the driest season the Alexandrians enjoy plentiful quantities of fresh water.

The City's Main Streets

While some visitors are fascinated by Alexandria's subterranean sectors, most focus their attention on what lies above ground. As many noted writers have pointed out, the view as seen from above the city would resemble a very large chlamys. "In plan," the first-century A.D. Roman scholar Pliny the Elder wrote, the town "is the shape of a Macedonian soldier's cloak, with indents in its circumference and projecting corners on the right and left sides."[8]

The city's main section lies on the narrow strip of land running between the sea in the north and Lake Mareotis in the south. This main section is dominated by two main streets. The longest is the Canopic Way, which runs east to west for a distance of more than twenty-four thousand feet (7,320 m), or almost five miles (8 km). The Sun Gate marks the eastern end of the Canopic Way, and the Moon Gate the western end. This street is one hundred feet wide, which allows several chariots and wagons, as well as large numbers of people, to use it simultaneously.

The other main avenue—the Street of the Soma—is also one hundred feet wide. It bisects the Canopic Way in the west-central part of the city, meeting the other street at a right angle. Located at their junction is a square—the

The World's Most Splendid City?

A number of historians and travelers have described Alexandria's unique and splendid layout, including the first-century B.C. Greek Diodorus Siculus. This excerpt is from volume eight of his Library of History.

[Alexander] gave orders to . . . build the city between the marsh [Lake Mareotis] and the sea. He laid out the site and traced the streets skillfully. . . . By selecting the right angle of the streets, Alexander made the city breathe with the etesian winds, so that as these blow across a great expanse of sea, they cool the air of the town, and so he provided its inhabitants with a moderate climate and good health. Alexander also laid out the walls so that they were at once exceedingly large and marvelously strong. . . . In shape, it [the city] is similar to a *chlamys*, and it is approximately bisected by an avenue remarkable for its size and beauty. From gate to gate it runs a distance of [nearly five miles]; it is [one hundred feet] in width, and is bordered throughout its length with rich façades of houses and temples. . . . The city in general has grown so much in later times that many reckon it to be the first city of the civilized world, and it is certainly far ahead of all the rest in elegance and extent [size] and riches and luxury.

Soma—which contains the tomb of the city's illustrious founder. The city's other streets are laid out parallel to these two main streets, forming a convenient grid pattern. Another impressive feature of this layout is that the streets were designed to take advantage of the prevailing etesian winds, the northwestern winds that blow during the summer months. According to the first-century B.C. Greek historian Diodorus Siculus, Alexander and his architect

> laid out the site and traced the streets skillfully. . . . By selecting the right angle of the streets, Alexander made the city breathe with the ete-

sian winds, so that as these blow across a great expanse of sea, they cool the air of the town, and so he provided its inhabitants with a moderate climate and good health.[9]

Both the Canopic Way and Street of the Soma are lined with important and impressive buildings. At the Canopic Way's far eastern end, just outside the city's defensive wall, lies the racetrack, which the Greeks call a hippodrome and the Romans a circus. This is where chariot and horse races are held. Entering the city gate and walking westward along the Canopic Way, one comes to a smaller stadium located on the north side of

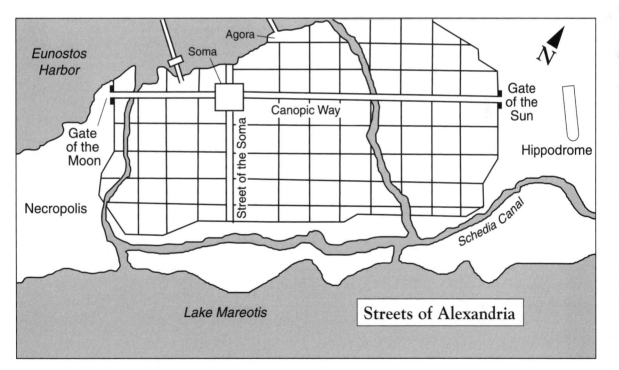

Streets of Alexandria

During a race held in the hippodrome, just outside the city's eastern wall, a charioteer moves to block another driver who is trying to seize the lead.

the street. This stadium is for Greek-style athletic games. Across the street from the stadium is a large gymnasium complex, where many Alexandrian men go to exercise, wrestle, and relax. Farther west of these buildings one sees the magnificent Museum and Great Library on the left, and still farther west lies the amphitheater, where gladiatorial combats take place, and the temples of the gods Saturn and Pan. In addition to these prominent landmarks, the two streets are lined with tall marble colonnades (rows of columns), stone sphinxes, statues, and other monuments.

The Causeway and Harbors

Running along the northern side of the city, parallel to the Canopic Way, are the shores of the two Alexandrian harbors. Originally, of course, one unbroken shoreline faced the Pharos Island. But Alexander's engineers built a causeway of stone and dirt about 4,200 feet (1,280 m) long, connecting the island to the city proper. That causeway is called the Heptastadion.[10] It both enlarged the city and divided one ill-defined harbor area into two well-defined, conveniently sheltered bays. An open archway, the "Slipway," located in the Heptastadion's northern end, near the Pharos, allows small ships to pass from one bay to the other. (Carts, mules, and people access the Pharos via a bridge that passes over the Slipway.)

The first of these bays, the eastern, or Great Harbor, is a roughly circular area about a mile and a half wide. Its outline is delineated by the curving western end of the Pharos Island, the Heptastadion, the shoreline of the north-

ern section of the city, and a narrow peninsula—the Lochias—extending outward from the city's eastern end. The harbor features a series of wide, well-maintained docks near the base of the Heptastadion. These served as the home base for the Ptolemaic royal war fleets, while royal yachts, including Cleopatra's famous pleasure barge, moored at separate docks located in a small inlet on the harbor's southeastern shore, near the royal palaces. Roman warships and cargo transports now use many of these docks.

The western harbor, or Eunostos, is a port linking the city to the important trade route leading into Egypt's interior. On the south shore of the Eunostos

Strabo Describes Alexandria

Strabo (64 B.C.–ca.A.D.24), the great Greek geographer, provided one of the best written overviews of Alexandria. Here, from volume eight of his Geography, *he describes the harbors, canal, cemetery, and other prominent sights in the western sector of the city.*

The harbor of Eunostos comes after the Heptastadion, and above this the artificial harbor which they call *Kibotos* [the Box], which also includes dockyards. Further in is a navigable canal which connects with Lake Mareotis. Beyond the canal there is only a small part of the city. Then comes the [region] of Necropolis, in which there are many gardens and tombs and installations suitable for the mummification of corpses. On the city side of the canal are the Serapeum [Temple of Serapis]. . . . The city is full of dedications and shrines. Finest of all is the gymnasium, the colonnades in the center of which are more than a stade [six hundred feet] in length, and also the Courts of Justice and the Groves. There is also the Paneion [Temple of Pan], an artificial circular mound in the shape of a fir-cone, resembling a rocky hill, with a spiral path to the summit; and from the top the whole city can be seen spread out beneath on all sides.

Cleopatra entertains Julius Caesar on her renowned pleasure barge. The two joined forces to depose her corrupt younger brother, Ptolemy XIII.

lies a small artificial, square-shaped harbor called the "Box," and on the southern side of the Box a canal crosses through the western sector of the city and connects with Lake Mareotis. Cargo ships from the outside world pass from the Eunostos into the Box, follow the canal to the lake, and then sail to ports on the lake's southern shores. There, goods are off-loaded for transport farther inland. In the same way, goods from the interior pass northward through this series of waterways and emerge into the Eunostos on their way to Mediterranean ports.

Pharos Island

The Pharos Island itself is the home of the great lighthouse, which stands on the island's eastern tip. There is much more to the Pharos, however. It is more than two miles long and nearly half a mile wide in the middle, with its own small harbor on the north side. It originally supported a good-sized village that, with the addition of the Heptastadion, became part of the city proper.

Unfortunately, though, most of the houses in this village were destroyed during the battles that took place there in 48 B.C. Julius Caesar had joined forces with the young Ptolemaic queen, Cleopatra, who was involved in a power struggle with her younger brother, Ptolemy XIII. The boy-king and his self-serving advisers wanted to depose Cleopatra and drive Caesar and his troops away. But though vastly outnumbered, Caesar outmaneuvered and defeated them. In his well-known war

journal, he himself described the situation on Pharos:

On the island there are houses where Egyptians live; in fact, there is a village almost big enough to be called a town. . . . While the enemy were fully engaged in fighting, I landed troops on Pharos, seized the place, and installed a garrison there.

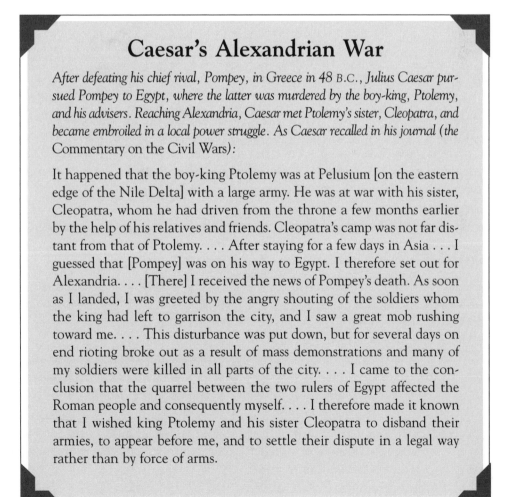

Caesar's Alexandrian War

After defeating his chief rival, Pompey, in Greece in 48 B.C., Julius Caesar pursued Pompey to Egypt, where the latter was murdered by the boy-king, Ptolemy, and his advisers. Reaching Alexandria, Caesar met Ptolemy's sister, Cleopatra, and became embroiled in a local power struggle. As Caesar recalled in his journal (the Commentary on the Civil Wars)*:*

It happened that the boy-king Ptolemy was at Pelusium [on the eastern edge of the Nile Delta] with a large army. He was at war with his sister, Cleopatra, whom he had driven from the throne a few months earlier by the help of his relatives and friends. Cleopatra's camp was not far distant from that of Ptolemy. . . . After staying for a few days in Asia . . . I guessed that [Pompey] was on his way to Egypt. I therefore set out for Alexandria. . . . [There] I received the news of Pompey's death. As soon as I landed, I was greeted by the angry shouting of the soldiers whom the king had left to garrison the city, and I saw a great mob rushing toward me. . . . This disturbance was put down, but for several days on end rioting broke out as a result of mass demonstrations and many of my soldiers were killed in all parts of the city. . . . I came to the conclusion that the quarrel between the two rulers of Egypt affected the Roman people and consequently myself. . . . I therefore made it known that I wished king Ptolemy and his sister Cleopatra to disband their armies, to appear before me, and to settle their dispute in a legal way rather than by force of arms.

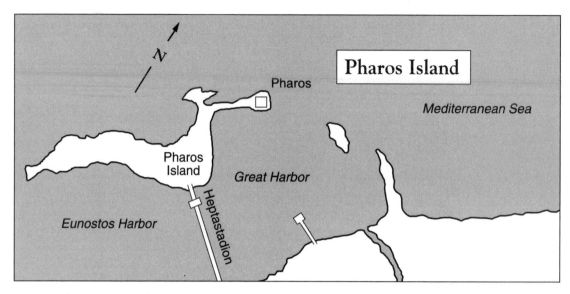

In this way I made sure of being able to receive supplies and reinforcements by sea.[11]

Since that time, the ruined village has remained largely abandoned. However, large numbers of people still frequent Pharos, including soldiers who man a small fort on the its south side, religious pilgrims visiting a temple honoring the goddess Isis, and tourists bound for the great lighthouse.

Outside the Walls

Finally, some mention must be made of the areas lying directly outside the city's walls. In the east, beyond the circus, lies the old necropolis (cemetery) used mainly in early Ptolemaic times. In the northern reaches of this sector, along the coast, one finds mostly Jewish tombs, as the city's Jewish quarter lies nearby. Farther east of the Jewish ceme-

tery, on a low hill overlooking the sea, lies the Roman military camp, which has been in almost constant use since Augustus's reign. And immediately to the south of the camp rests the soldiers' cemetery and a small temple where mourners stop to worship.

Beyond the city's western walls one will find the main necropolis, where most Alexandrians have buried their dead for at least the last two centuries. Most burials are in the style long prevalent in Athens and other parts of the Greek mainland. A well-to-do family will typically construct a *hypogaeum*, an elaborate underground tomb built of cut stone blocks, containing one to three chambers, and decorated with painted designs. Ordinary folk tend to inter their dead in small pits covered over with earth and small stone markers or altars. (By contrast, most native Egyptians living in the interior of the country wrap their dead in linen and bury them in makeshift graves dug in desert sands. Only a handful of upper-class Egyptians can afford tombs, each consisting of an underground chamber cut from stone or constructed of mud bricks.)

These descriptions of Alexandria's layout make clear what every visitor learns rather quickly. The city is logically constructed and self-contained, featuring every natural benefit and human facility necessary to keep its large population secure and comfortable. These include an ideal, pleasant climate; an easy-to-follow grid pattern for the streets; wide avenues to keep heavy traffic moving; numerous cisterns to collect life-giving water; two main harbors with ample docks; canals linking the city with inland fields and crops; and adequate cemeteries to bury the dead. In short, Alexandria is as comfortable and admirable a city as one will find anywhere in the known world.

CHAPTER THREE

Transportation, Lodging, and Food

Those inhabitants of various Mediterranean lands who wish to make the journey to Alexandria have few viable options. Passable roads do connect with the city. But these are few in number and located in only two regions—North Africa and Palestine. The North African road, which is fairly well maintained by the Roman government, runs along the coast from the western Mediterranean all the way to Alexandria. The trouble with this route is that it is very slow. Foot and wagon traffic from the heavily populated regions of North Africa (such as the city of Carthage) takes several weeks to reach the Nile Delta. Moreover, this road serves only a small portion of the empire's inhabitants, most of whom live along the sea's northern coasts.

The same can be said for the coastal road that enters Egypt from Palestine. It is well kept and certainly well traveled.

But it serves only travelers from the Near East. Also, this road does not connect directly with Alexandria, since one must cross the Nile River and its tributaries before making it to the city. So even from southern Palestine, which is relatively close to Egypt, a road trip to Alexandria can take up to a week or more.

The fastest and most convenient way for most people to reach Alexandria, therefore, is by ship. The journey from Rome usually takes no more than ten days. And one can reach Alexandria from Athens (actually its port of Piraeus) in six days, from Byzantium (near the mouth of the Black Sea) in nine days, and from Palestine in only two days.

Two reservations must be kept in mind, however. First, these optimistic time estimates assume that one is traveling in summer, when the etesian winds blow north to south across the Mediterranean, helping to propel ships toward Egypt. When these winds are

Planning the Trip

not blowing, one must expect such journeys to take longer. Second, ships making the return trip from Alexandria must often fight *against* these same winds. So the vessels tend to hug the coasts, stopping often in various ports and taking longer to get home. Still, even if the return trip to Athens takes ten or twelve days, overland travel by foot would take at least four to five weeks. Also, going by sea is considerably less strenuous and usually more pleasant than going by land.

For a fee, single-masted warships like this one sometimes carry civilian passengers from foreign ports to Alexandria.

In planning a voyage to Alexandria, the first consideration is finding a proper ship. Travelers must find space on a cargo vessel or other kind of ship that happens to be going to Egypt and book a passage. Cargo ships almost never follow a regular schedule. Prospective travelers must submit their names to a shipping company or boat captain in advance and wait patiently until the next departure. Sailing times can vary, depending on prevailing winds, financial problems, availability of crew, and other factors, and it is not unusual for a captain to decide to leave on a moment's notice. So travelers often must wait near the docks for days, and sometimes weeks, to ensure that the boat does not sail without them.

One's chances of finding a timely,

The Alexandrian Grain Ships

Each year many huge grain ships make the round trips from Alexandria to Rome and Alexandria to Athens, carrying hundreds of passengers as well as enormous amounts of cargo. For those travelers who have not had the opportunity of seeing one of these great ships up close, the popular Greek writer Lucian provides this description (from The Ship *in volume six of his complete works):*

What a size the ship was! 180 feet in length, the ship's carpenter told me, the beam more than a quarter of that, and 44 feet from the deck to the lowest point in the hold. And the height of the mast, and what a yard it carried, and what a forestay held it up! . . . Everything was incredible: the rest of the decoration, the paintings, the red topsail, even more, the anchors with their capstans and winches, and the cabins [for the crew] aft [in the rear]. The crew was like an army. They told me she carried enough grain to feed every mouth in Athens for a year. And it all depended for its safety on one little old man who turns those great steering oars with a tiller that's no more than a stick! They pointed him out to me; wooly-haired little fellow, half-bald. Heron was his name, I think.

This huge grainship, converted from a warship, often carries passengers too.

reliable, and fast ship increase with the size of the vessel. Small cargo ships, warships, ferries, and the like have room for only a few passengers. And these vessels tend to hug the coasts and make frequent stops. The best bet for the voyage to Alexandria is a large cargo ship, especially one of the huge ships that carry Egyptian grain to Rome and other major Mediterranean ports. Some of these are 180 feet in length, and they can accommodate as many as six hundred travelers in addition to their cargoes! Moreover, they make the round trip from Alexandria to Rome and back fairly often during the prime sailing season from April to October.

Having found the right ship, the traveler's next step is to secure an exit pass from the port of departure. Not all ports require such passes. But many do, including Alexandria itself, a reality travelers will have to deal with when they are ready to leave that city. (Tourists are not alone in this regard; merchants and even the captains and crews of cargo and other vessels must also obtain passes.)

So be prepared to get a pass and also to pay the fee that accompanies it. One must apply in writing to the Roman governor. He then authorizes an Alexandrian port official to issue the pass and collect the fee, which varies according to one's profession, status, and sometimes gender. The captain of a merchant ship usually pays eight drachmas. (To get an idea of how much money this represents, keep in mind that an ordinary laborer makes between one and two drachmas per day and a skilled one about twice that amount.) The ship's crewmen pay a fee of five drachmas; skilled laborers eight; unskilled laborers three to five; wives of soldiers twenty; and prostitutes one hundred or more. (The higher fees for women, especially prostitutes, are meant to discourage them from leaving the city, where their "services" are much in demand.)

A group of Athenian nobles approach the main docks at Alexandria. Most are excited because it is their first trip to the city.

Units of Currency

The money system used in Alexandria is based on the Greek drachma. Some coins or monetary units are smaller fractions of the drachma, while specific numbers of drachmas combine to make larger units. The main units are as follows: Six obols equal one drachma; one hundred drachmas equal one mina; and sixty minae (or six thousand drachmas) equal one talent. Take note that minas and talents are represented by weights of silver rather than by coins. Some non-standard but fairly common coins include the didrachm (equal to two drachmas), tetradrachm (four drachmas), pentadrachm (five drachmas), and diobol (two obols). The Roman denarius, an extremely common coin in the Mediterranean world outside of Alexandria, is usually roughly equated with the tetradrachm.

The Sea Voyage

When it is time to board the ship, travelers should make sure that they have all the necessary items for eating, bathing, and sleeping, as well as dressing. Most travelers must sleep on deck in makeshift beds made out of whatever they can carry. Small tents for privacy and protection from rain are common. But ship captains insist that they be erected each evening and dismantled each morning. Most good-sized ships have galleys equipped with a hearth for cooking. Typically, the crew has first use of the galley and any passengers must wait their turn; they must also supply their own foods, pots and pans, eating utensils, and so forth. It is advisable also to bring along a pot for relieving oneself (which one empties over the side).

Travelers must also bring along some means of passing the time during the voyage, as the crew's job is to operate the ship, not to entertain passengers. Books, dice, knucklebones, and other gambling items are common. One must be very careful, however, not to engage in any activity that the captain and crew would look on as a bad omen. Dancing is forbidden, for example, as it is thought to anger certain gods. Swearing, even in writing, is also taboo. If someone dies during the trip, their body is thrown overboard because death at sea is a very bad omen. And travelers should not cut their nails or hair, except when a storm is approaching; then throwing these clippings in the water may help avert disaster.

Speaking of storms, all travelers are warned that such events are unpredictable and are bound to happen from time to time. Unless one's boat capsizes in midsea, the chances of surviving a storm are good, but it is nevertheless a harrowing experience. A Greek resident of Alexandria was caught in a bad storm off the Egyptian coast and later described it in a letter to his brother:

> The men groaned, the women shrieked, everybody called upon the gods, cried aloud, remembered their dear ones. Only Amarantus was in good spirits, thinking he was going to get out of paying his creditors. . . . I noticed that the soldiers had all drawn their swords. I asked why and learned that they preferred to belch up their souls to the open air, on the deck, rather than gurgle them up to the sea [i.e., they would rather commit suicide than drown]. . . . Then someone called out that all who had any gold should hang it around their neck. Those who had [some gold] did so. . . . The women not only put on their jewelry but handed out pieces of string to any who needed them [to tie jewelry and money to their bodies]. This is a time-honored practice, and the reason for it is this: you must provide the corpse of someone lost at sea with the money to pay for a

This large well-kept house, located on a quiet side street in Alexandria, is one of many local private homes that will rent a room to a respectable traveler.

funeral so that whoever recovers it . . . won't mind [giving the body a proper burial]. . . . The ship was rushing along under full canvas because we couldn't shorten sail. Time and again we laid hands on the lines but gave up because they were jammed in the blocks. And secretly we began to be equally afraid that, even if we escaped from the raging sea, we would be approaching land in the dead of night in this helpless condition. Day broke before this happened, and we saw the sun—and never with greater pleasure. . . . When we touched beloved land, we embraced it like a living mother.[12]

Waiting for an Exit Pass

The wait for an exit pass, or the permission from the local authorities to sail from a port, can sometimes take a long time and become tedious or frustrating for merchants and other travelers. This letter (quoted in Select Papyri*), written in Rome by an Alexandrian business-man to his brother back home, is a case in point:*

Dear Apollinarius: Many greetings. I pray continuously for your health. I am well. I'm writing to let you know that I reached the land [Italy] on June 30 and that we unloaded [at Rome's port of Ostia] on July 12. I went up to Rome on the 19th and the place welcomed us as the gods wished. We are daily expecting our sailing papers; up to today, not one of the grain fleet has been cleared. Best regards to your wife . . . and all your friends. Good-bye. Your brother Irenaeus. August 2.

Finding Suitable Lodgings

Assuming travelers have avoided any such mishaps during the voyage, the first aspect of Alexandria they will see will be the pinnacle of the famous Pharos lighthouse as it rises above the horizon in the distance. It is visible from many miles out at sea and is always an awesome sight. Soon the entire structure, as well as other Alexandrian buildings, comes into view. Finally, the ship enters the western harbor and docks there, as first-time visitors peer shoreward in excited anticipation.

Having disembarked, travelers' best course of action is to find a place to stay before attempting any sightseeing. The city offers several different kinds of lodgings with a wide range of facilities and prices. For those who can afford it, several expensive resort hotels can be found just outside the city walls along the canal that carries water from the Nile's Canopic branch. A typical version is a two-story structure about seventy feet long and forty feet wide, although some are much larger. The rooms line and face inward into a large

This spacious, well-to-do house owned by a Roman merchant rents two of its rooms to visiting businessmen and other travelers of means.

central courtyard that is open to the sky and affords an inflow of pleasant breezes. Each room has at least one window. And the hotel features communal amenities such as a large kitchen, one or more dining rooms, a storage area for wagons and carriages, a stable for horses and other animals, and private baths, which feature hot and cold pools in which to cleanse oneself and relax. The very best hotels also have snack bars, exercise and massage rooms, and reading rooms.

Inside the city walls, travelers will find many smaller, less expensive hotels and inns. Some have central courtyards, while others lack this amenity. Most of the less expensive inns have smaller, more cramped rooms, many of

Typical Household Goods

The Alexandrian townhouses that rent rooms to visitors must be well furnished and well equipped to provide convenience and comfort to both members of the host family and their guests. This inventory of goods from such a household (quoted in Naphtali Lewis's Life in Egypt Under Roman Rule) *is illustrative:*

In the cellar: basin, bronze, 1; tankard, tin, 1; cup, tin, 1; wooden measure, ironclad, 1; small washtub, 1; lampstand, bronze, with shade, 1. In the storerooms: small dish, tin, 1; cups and saucers, tin, 3; small lamp, bronze, 1; cloak, gold-colored, 1. . . . In the upper rooms: kettle, bronze, 1; cup, tin, 1; saucepan, bronze, 1; small colander, bronze, 1; mixing bowls, 2; pruning knives, 3; dish, tin, 1; pitcher, bronze, 1; measure, bronze, 1; wooden measures, ironclad, 2; cloaks, gold-colored, 3 . . . pillows, green, 2 . . . mattresses, stuffed, 2; bedcover, 1; couch, 1; chest, 1; small storage box, bronze, 1.

which have no windows. These places usually supply candles or oil lamps, but some do not; so the traveler is advised to carry along one or the other, as the room might otherwise be pitch-black. Such establishments most often lack eating facilities and baths, although this presents no problem, since restaurants and bathhouses can be found all over the city.

Those travelers who cannot afford or for some reason do not want to stay at hotels and inns can avail themselves of private lodgings. Some owners of private townhouses rent out rooms, which are as a rule less expensive than the ones at the inns. Owners usually hang out signs or plaques to advertise. These can be quite clever or charming, as in the following example: "If you're clean and neat, then there's a house ready and waiting for you. If you're dirty—well, I'm ashamed to say it, but you're welcome too."[13]

As might be expected, such townhouses vary in size and luxury. The largest are two to three stories high and have central courtyards, making them look somewhat like miniature versions of the larger hotels. The courtyard of such a house usually features a well to supply fresh water, although it might also tap into one of the cisterns that run beneath the city. The owners' bedrooms, as well as the kitchen and dining room, are usually found on the first floor. Servants' quarters and extra bedrooms, which are offered to travelers, are on the second floor. (The third floor, if there is one, is generally a storage space.) The visitor can sometimes strike a deal in which the owner provides kitchen privileges along with the room, all for one price; otherwise, the traveler must eat out at a restaurant.

Eating Establishments

Fortunately, eating places are plentiful in Alexandria. If one is looking for something simple and quick, there are hundreds of small fast food and drink establishments; the Greeks usually refer to them as taverns (*kapeleia*), while the Romans call them cookshops (*thermopolii*). Some are mainly drinking places that provide only snacks, such as figs, cheese, pastries, and sometimes bread and porridge. The Roman-style cookshops have a much wider fare, including hot food. Such cookshops are hard to miss, as they typically have a marble-topped counter opening right into the sidewalk; customers walk up to the counter and order, after which they can either stand and eat or take the food back to their rooms. The cooking is done on a metal grill over a small charcoal furnace recessed into the counter. Recently cooked food, such as sausages and other grilled meats, stays warm in ceramic jars. Bread, cheese, figs, dates, nuts, cakes, and of course wine are also available. Taverns and cookshops are most numerous in the city's main marketplace, located south of the eastern harbor docks, but quite a few can be found in other sections of town, as well as in or near the hotels lining the Canopus canal.

If visitors are looking for a sit-down meal, they should look for a regular restaurant. Many such establishments have street-side counters, like the cookshops, but they also feature one or more small dining rooms equipped with tables

Pictured here is a well-carved relief sculpture of a local shop. The owner and his son display some of their wares, including a wide array of fine knives, cleavers, and other tools.

In this painting on an elegant vase for sale in an Alexandrian shop, a woman of high social station holds a platter containing figs, cheese, pastries, and other tasty snacks.

and chairs. A few more elaborate versions have private dining rooms, latrines, and also couches around the tables for those who prefer to recline, rather than sit, while eating. Some restaurants provide entertainment, too. Musicians, dancing girls, and occasionally jugglers and other specialty acts are fairly common attractions.

Food and Drink

Because Alexandria is a wealthy city and lies at the crossroads of trade routes from both eastern and western lands, the foods available in many restaurants are diverse, sometimes even exotic. Standard fare includes bread, barley porridge, cakes and other pastries, cheese, yogurt, fruit (including figs, dates, grapes, and currants), eggs, olives, vegetables (including beans, lentils, peas, lettuce, onions, beets, cucumbers, and mushrooms), fish and shellfish, fowl (including ducks, geese, pigeons, owls, larks, jays, and nightingales, many of these imported), and the meats of lamb, deer, boar, and rabbit. For those who can afford it, delicacies such as lobster, pheasant, ostrich, peacocks and peacock brains, flamingo tongues, gazelles, and fish livers are available in a number of eating establishments. (Note: Those contemplating taking side trips into the Egyptian interior should be aware that such exotic foods are harder to find and much more expensive outside of Alexandria.)

No matter how well prepared, none of these dishes would be complete without the proper beverage to accompany them. Those visiting from foreign lands should note that wine is the main drink in Alexandria (as well as in Athens, Rome, and other parts of the Mediterranean world). Some wine is made locally from grapes grown at vineyards in the Nile Delta; but much is imported from Palestine, Syria, and Greece. Following ancient Greco-Roman custom, almost all Alexandrians mix their wine with water in a large bowl called a *crater*, then ladle it into goblets. Drinking undiluted wine is seen as undignified or even uncivilized. Many people sweeten their wine with honey, while poorer folk often drink *posca*, a mixture of water and a low-quality, vinegar-like wine. In addition to grape-based

Spices from Around the World

The cooks in the better Alexandrian restaurants are world renowned for some of their dishes. To no small degree this is due to their use of various tasty combinations of spices to make their fare more appetizing. No other city, with the possible exception of Rome, attracts traders from all parts of the known world; so a wide range of spices are imported for use in Alexandrian kitchens. Only a partial list includes salt, pepper, ginger, balsam, cinnamon, sweet marjoram, myrrh, cassia, frankincense, rue, mint, and parsley. Some of these are added to the recipes before cooking; others are sprinkled onto cooked food just prior to serving; and still others are employed in making tangy sauces.

These Egyptian brewers are making henket, *the country's popular and tasty traditional beer.*

wines, those made from figs, dates, and pomegranates are available at many taverns, as well as in the marketplace.

Beer is almost as popular as wine in Alexandria, as in other parts of Egypt. Two types are available. One, the least common and popular here, is a Romano-Celtic variety imported from central Europe. The other is Egyptian beer (*henket*). Barley, emmer wheat, or a mixture of the two is combined with water and allowed to ferment; then honey, date juice, and/or various spices are added for extra flavoring. Egyptian beer constitutes a major portion of the diet of poorer native Egyptians living outside of Alexandria. It is not surprising, therefore, that many foreign visitors with minimal funds tend to drink a lot of beer during their stay in this extraordinary city.

CHAPTER FOUR

Shopping, Comerce, and Industry

Next to Rome, Alexandria is the greatest trading center in the world. In fact, the Alexandrians themselves consider their city to be *the* center of world commerce. Merchants regularly arrive from many lands, near and far, carrying an incredible range of products, some that remain in Alexandria and others that continue on to other cities. Only a partial list of these products includes the following: from Carthage and North Africa, wheat, lions and other wild animals for the arena games, oil for lamps, and ivory and citrus wood for making fine furniture; from Sicily, pork and fine aged cheeses; from Spain, gold, silver, tin, and horses; from Gaul,[14] copper pots and pans, pottery dishes, fine wines, and furry animal hides; from Rhodes and other Aegean islands, fuller's earth for finishing and cleaning

This beautiful red-figure vase was imported from Athens.

clothes; from cities along the shores of the Black Sea, wheat and other grains; from mainland Greece, copper, pottery vases and cups, horses, honey, statues, and paintings; from Asia Minor, wool and carpets; from Nubia and Sudan (African lands south of Egypt), elephants, gold, and spices; from Palestine, dates and other fruits; from Syria, spices, glassware, and fine textiles; from Arabia, perfumes and spices; from faraway India, precious gems and fine textiles; and from the even more distant, fabled region of China, silks and spices.

Samples of this tremendous array of goods make their way from the docks in Alexandria's western and eastern harbors to shops across the city. These shops also contain examples of the many foodstuffs, textiles, jewelry, glass-

ware, pottery items, and other fine products made in the city itself. So the combination of native and imported goods makes shopping in Alexandria a worthwhile and, in the opinion of many visitors, exciting experience.

Exchanging Money

Before beginning to shop, however, travelers must make sure that they have the proper currency. The standard accepted unit of currency is the Greek drachma, originally introduced into Egypt by the early Ptolemaic kings. (The Ptolemies issued their own distinct version of the drachma; other versions were generally not accepted in Egypt.) Before that, the native Egyptians did not use coins; instead, they engaged in barter, exchanging

Opening the Trade Route to India

One of the greatest achievements of the Ptolemaic regime was the opening of a trade route to faraway India. It happened partly by chance and partly through the skill and courage of a Greek sea captain named Eudoxos. During the reign of Ptolemy VII (who earned the nickname "Sausage" because he was so fat), an Indian sailor washed ashore on the African coast of the Red Sea. When he had learned enough Greek to communicate, he explained that his cargo ship had been wrecked in a storm and he offered to guide a Ptolemaic ship to his homeland. The king hired Eudoxos, who subsequently succeeded in reaching India several times. During these voyages, he discovered the monsoon winds; these blow across the Arabian Sea from the northeast to the southwest for half the year and the other way during the other half, making the trip to India fairly easy if timed correctly. Eudoxos later went to Spain and attempted to sail around the African continent. But the attempt must have failed, for he was never heard from again.

This tetradrachm, worth four drachmas, bears the image of Alexandria's illustrious founder, Alexander III.

various goods for other goods. The transition to regular currency was difficult for the natives, some of whom, especially in the country's interior sections, took several generations to adjust. However, the Alexandrians adapted quickly, partly because so many of them were Greek and already used to dealing in drachmas.

Thus, visitors with foreign coins, bronze ingots, jewelry, or other valuable modes of payment will need to exchange them for drachmas. One alternative is to go to a local temple that does such exchanges. The standard charge for doing the exchange is 6 percent, though it can sometimes be higher.

Much more common are private bankers who act as money changers; indeed, they set up their tables outside temples and on practically every corner and square in the marketplace. (Their Greek name—*trapezitai*—translates literally as "table-men." The Romans call them *argentarii* and their tables *mensa publica*.) They carefully weigh all coins and other valuables and are very adept at spotting phony gold and silver coins.

Bankers also provide other financial services. They loan money, for example, often to ship owners and other merchants, but also to ordinary people for all manner of needs. If one is fortunate, he might find a banker willing to lend at an interest rate of 8 to 10 percent per year. However, some charge the legal limit—1 percent a month, or 12 percent a year. (Still, this is far more equitable than the situation under the Ptolemies, who, by royal decree, allowed lenders to charge as much as 24 percent per year!) Bankers also take money and other valuables on deposit; buy, sell, and manage land and buildings for people; and collect outstanding debts for a fee (usually a percentage of the debt collected).

Navigating the Agora

Once visitors have secured the proper currency, they are ready to begin shopping. Shops and vendors of numerous kinds can be found all over

A Banker's Oath

Many of the bankers in Ptolemaic times worked for the royal government, which benefited from the revenues gained from exchanging money, making loans, and collecting taxes. These bankers were all Greeks appointed by the palace, but their assistants were often native Egyptians. The assistants had to take an oath of office, like this one [quoted in Naphtali Lewis's Greeks in Ptolemaic Egypt]:

In the reign of Ptolemy [III Euergetes], son of Ptolemy [II Philadelphus] . . . [an] oath sworn . . . [by] Herakleopolis, [a banker's] assistant. . . . I swear by King Ptolemy . . . and by the sibling gods and the benefactor gods and their ancestors . . . that I will assuredly serve under Klitarchos, agent of the banker Asklepiades. . . . I will duly and truly deposit all money that I receive from Klitarchos, except for my salary, to the bank['s main office]. . . . If any expenditure which I make in the field is authorized, I will give to Klitarchos an account of all payments . . . and receipts for whatever I spend; if I owe anything [at the end of] my period of service, I will pay it to the royal bank within five days . . . and I shall be available to Klitarchos and his agents outside sanctuary, altar, temple precinct and every [other] protection. If I abide by my oath, may it go well with me; if I violate my oath, may I be liable for sacrilege.

Alexandria, but the vast majority are concentrated in the marketplace, or agora. This is a large area sandwiched between the eastern harbor docks (behind the rows of warehouses) and the eastern flank of the Street of the Soma.

Around the perimeter of the agora stretches a series of long, low buildings, each with an open side that faces inward into the center of the marketplace. The Greek name for such a building is a stoa, the basic design for which originated in mainland Greece. One walks under a roofed porch supported by a row of columns on the open side of the building. There one finds rows of shops, one beside the other, forming a sort of shopping mall. The stoas, as well as many small buildings that adjoin them, also contain taverns, cookshops, small inns, industrial workshops, and other businesses.

In the central part of the agora, many portable shops can be found. Each usually consists of one or two wagons filled with the vendor's goods, which can vary from fruits and vegetables to textiles to figurines and all manner of things. Such a portable shop is typically covered by awnings or in some cases a tent to protect the owner and his customers from rain and the hot sun.

Merchants consider certain sections of the agora, such as the strip facing the Street of the Soma, to be more lucrative than others; so verbal and even physical disputes sometimes erupt over who has the right to the better spots. Luckily, the governor has an official in charge of overseeing markets (including making sure that the scales used by merchants are accurate), and he and his men are able to settle most such disputes with a minimum of injury.

The Local Metalworking Industry

Although many of the items visitors buy in the agora are imported from around the world, quite a few are manufactured in the city, often in the agora itself. One of the most famous goldsmiths in the world, for instance, has a workshop there. In fact, the gold and silver objects made in the city have been world renowned since early Ptolemaic times, when Alexandrian metalworkers turned out magnificent treasures for the royal family and the wealthy elite. These included statues of the Greek goddess Nike (Victory) with solid gold wings; gold and silver

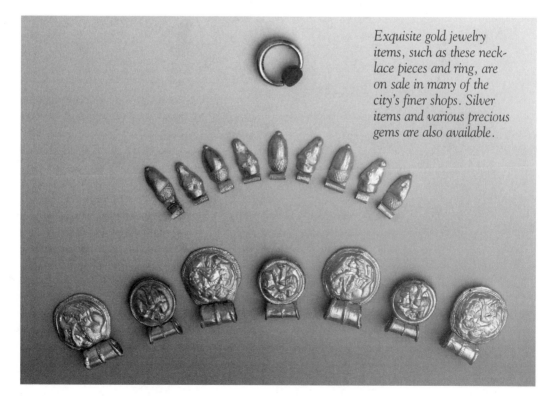

Exquisite gold jewelry items, such as these necklace pieces and ring, are on sale in many of the city's finer shops. Silver items and various precious gems are also available.

jewelry and crowns; and mixing bowls, altars, tripods, cups, pitchers, and other objects coated with gold or silver leaf.

Locally made gold and silver jewelry and bowls are still popular items in Alexandrian shops. (Some of the local work is manufactured in small workshops in the Delta and also in Memphis. Many of the artisans in Memphis are called Hellenomenphites, reflecting their mixed Greek and Egyptian heritage.) Tourists can sometimes watch the local artisans as they work these precious metals. They start with ingots (bars) and beat

Hollow-Casting Bronze

In addition to simple molding and the lost wax technique, bronze workers often employ the more complex hollow-casting method, which allows them to make larger, hollow bronze objects such as busts and statues (solid versions being too expensive and heavy). The workers make a clay core, surround it with a wax model of the object desired, then cover the wax with more clay. When fired, the wax melts, leaving a hollow space with the dimensions and details of the original model. They then pour bronze into the hollow and later remove the clay.

them with hammers into thin sheets. Eventually, they hammer the sheets so that they conform to the shape of stone molds of the desired objects, or else they cut the sheets into thin strips, some of them wirelike, to make chains and earrings. The hammer marks and rough edges are later polished away. For solid gold or silver items, the workers melt the metals and cast them in hollow stone molds.

Though not as precious as gold and silver, bronze is popular and widely used for dinnerware, serving vessels, figurines, lamp stands, brooches, and many other items. (Bronze models of the Pharos lighthouse, Temple of Serapis, and other Alexandrian landmarks are widely available in various sizes and remain popular with tourists.) Alexandrian metalworkers employ a variety of casting (molding) techniques. The simplest one is to pour melted bronze into a stone mold, allow it to dry, and then remove the mold. Another, the "lost wax" method, involves making a wax model of the object desired, then covering it with clay. When fired in an oven, the clay hardens, but the wax melts away; the bronze is poured into the resulting hollow space, and when the metal solidifies, the clay is removed.

Alexandria's Famous Glassware

Glassmaking skills came to Alexandria from Syria in the fourth century B.C., in

These magnificent glass containers were made by a Roman artisan whose father moved to Alexandria and opened a shop.

early Ptolemaic times, and the city soon became the principal center of production for the entire Mediterranean world. Alexandrian glassware is regularly exported to Rome and most of its many provinces. And to the delight of legions of visitors each year, many shops in Alexandria carry glass items that can be found nowhere else.

Even if one cannot afford to buy Alexandrian glassware, which can be quite expensive, all visitors are urged to visit a local glassmaking workshop. Without doubt, it is a fascinating and memorable experience. The glassmaker forms molten (hot liquid) glass around a core of mud or some other material. When the glass cools, he carefully removes the core. Of course, consistency of shape and thickness is difficult to achieve using this technique; so, few artisans are able to master it. The newer method—glassblowing—invented in the first century B.C., greatly reduces the difficulties of the traditional technique. Glass jars, bottles, bowls, perfume flasks, and so forth can be made faster, larger, and cheaper, though they are still elegant and beautiful.

Clear glass items became the rage near the close of the last century and remain the style most in demand. However, every shop carries some samples of colored glass, which were more popular than the clear variety in prior centuries. Colored glass is made by deliberately adding certain impurities to the molten glass—such as cobalt for a deep blue color, copper for greenish-blues and reds, manganese for pinks and purples, and so on. Also popular are cut and engraved glass items; be warned that the more elaborate versions are extremely expensive.

Pottery, Textiles, and Perfumes

Among the other distinctive products made and sold in Alexandria, as well as widely exported from the city, are pottery (ceramics), textiles, and perfumes. Alexandrian potters employ more or less the same methods as potters elsewhere. A few work the wet clay by hand or press it into hollow molds and allow it to dry; among the more popular items made this way are models of the Pharos lighthouse and some of the city's other famous structures. However, most potters work the clay on wheels that spin when the operator presses a foot pedal. This is the chief method for making vases, cups, bowls, pitchers, decorative plates, and other such vessels.

The two most distinctive and popular local ceramic styles are black-glazed and Hadra. Black-glazed vases are ribbed and feature black floral decorations on a white background. The Hadra vases are of two varieties. The first features decorative panels applied in black on a pale brown layer of terracotta (baked clay); the other has a painted white background on which are painted multicolored images of shields, swords, altars, and the like. Faience (pottery coated with colored glazes) is also quite popular in Alexandria. Lamps, bowls, vases, statuettes, and other items with the city's characteristic apple-green glaze are exported to many other cities. In addition, Alexandrian shops carry a wide range of ceramics imported from Greece, Italy, Asia Minor, and other regions.

Like so many other fine products made and sold in the city, Alexandrian textiles first became famous under the early Ptolemies. Artisans employed by the royal family and courtiers created magnificent clothes, and Ptolemaic military officers sported cloaks bearing portraits of members of the royal family, as well as detailed mythological scenes. Today, elegant carpets, hanging tapestries, bedspreads, and clothes of all types are in demand both as exports and in local shops.

Alexandria is also world-famous for its fine perfumes, which make excellent gifts. These scents are distilled from aromatic gums in a time-consuming process. The gums come mainly from Somalia (in eastern Africa), Arabia, and India; and because some of these lands are so distant and require long, expensive voyages to reach, such perfumes are likewise expensive. Cheaper varieties, made from local gums and flowering plants, are available for shoppers of lesser means.

Papyrus and Books

Perhaps the most distinctively Egyptian of all the products on sale in Alexandrian shops are papyrus and books. The city's merchants, as well as Egyptian merchants in general, benefit from the fact that most of the reading materials, letters, treatises, and public documents used in the Empire are written on paper made from papyrus. Indeed, this marsh plant native to Egypt is widely acknowledged to be a crucial

This is a red-figure ceramic vase imported from Athens. Alexandria's shops also feature imports from many other Greek cities.

asset of Mediterranean society as a whole. In the words of Pliny the Elder: "Our civilization—or at any rate our written records—depend especially on the use of paper."[15]

The process of making such paper is ingenious. Pliny supplies the following concise description:

Paper is manufactured from papyrus by splitting it [the plant's stem] with a needle into strips that are very thin but as long as possible. The quality of the papyrus is best at the center of the plant and decreases progressively toward the outsides. . . . All paper is "woven" on a board dampened with water from the Nile [to prevent the strips from drying out]; the muddy liquid acts as glue. First, an upright layer is smeared on the table—the whole length of the papyrus is used and both its ends are trimmed; then strips are laid across and complete a criss-cross pattern, which is then squeezed in presses. The sheets are dried in the sun and then joined together.[16]

When joined edge to edge by glue, about twenty papyrus sheets are wound around a wooden dowel, making a roll usually twenty or thirty feet long. People write on the papyrus with a reed or bronze pen dipped in ink made from carbon black (soot). A single long work

Scholars study some of the thousands of papyrus books in the Alexandrian library's vast collection. It is by far the largest library in the known world.

Pastes Used in Making Paper

In his massive work, the Natural History, *the noted Roman scholar Pliny the Elder gives this informative description of the adhesives used in the manufacture of paper from sheets of dried papyrus.*

A basic paste is made from the finest-quality flour mixed with boiling water and a sprinkling of vinegar; carpenter's paste and gum are too brittle an adhesive. A still better method of making paste is to mix breadcrumbs in boiling water. This results in the least amount of paste at the joins and produces paper softer even than linen. All pastes used should be just a day old, neither more or less. When pasted, the paper is beaten thin with a mallet and its surface covered with paste; once more it has its creases removed by pressure and is flattened with a mallet.

often consists of several rolled books. Blank papyrus rolls are sold in many Alexandrian shops, as are all manner of complete books (copied by hand) by writers from numerous lands. Of course, by far the largest collection of books in the city, or anywhere else, rests in Alexandria's Great Library, and the city is widely acknowledged to be the literary capital of the world.

Also available in shops is a newer, somewhat more durable kind of book that has not yet replaced the papyrus variety but perhaps will someday. It fea-tures a parchment called vellum, a tough material made from the skin of cattle, goats, or sheep. Vellum is made into sheets, each sheet becoming a page of a book, called a codex. The pages are stitched to a thin spine and bound with thin wooden boards.[17]

Though expensive, books, like gold jewelry, bronze figurines, fine ceramics, and perfumes, make wonderful gifts. It is no wonder that hundreds of books are sold in Alexandria each year to visitors taking advantage of perhaps the world's greatest shopping experience.

Temples and Gods

From the days of Alexandria's founding, religious worship of the eternal gods has been an irreplaceable pillar of the community. As the Greek historian Arrian told it, the founder, the great Alexander, "himself designed the general layout of the new town, indicating . . . the number of temples to be built, and what gods they should serve—the gods of Greece and the Egyptian Isis."[18] Here, Greek and Egyptian gods are mentioned in the same breath, and indeed, that was and remains a major key to the city's success—that it respects and combines elements of the belief systems of all sectors of the population. This is true not only of the Greek and Egyptian deities. The gods and temples of the Romans, Jews, and others have at one time or another been incorporated into Alexandrian religious society. And that has helped to foster and perpetuate the city's cosmopolitan, largely tolerant atmosphere.

Serapis and the Kiss of the Sun

Perhaps in no other instance has this fusion of religious diversity been more pronounced than in the foundation of the cult of Serapis (or Sarapis). In the early years of the Ptolemaic monarchy, King Ptolemy I Soter sought various ways to create a harmonious relationship between his Egyptian and Greek subjects. One of the most effective ways was to introduce the worship of a god that had qualities all could appreciate, regardless of ethnic and religious background. So he sent for a statue of a god worshiped by the people of the city of Sinope (on the Black Sea's southern shore), and he made that new god—Serapis—the symbol of Alexandrian religious devotion and tolerance.

Serapis became almost instantly popular, not only in Alexandria, but throughout Egypt, and in time his worship spread to many other cities in the Mediterranean world, including Rome. Part of Serapis's popularity stems from the fact that he embodies qualities with which most people can readily relate. Native Egyptians, for instance, view Serapis essentially as a version of their traditional god Osiris, who symbolizes fertility and new life.

As the cult of Serapis gained in popularity, it became clear that the god had to have a proper temple. So Ptolemy I began work on the structure, which his grandson, Ptolemy III (who reigned from 246 to 221 B.C.), completed. It became known as the Serapeum (or Serapeion), in honor of the god himself. The builders chose a commanding site, the acropolis (rocky hill) rising in the southwestern sector of the city just west of the Street of the Soma and just south of the Canopic Way. Here, it is clearly visible from all parts of the city, as well as from well out to sea.

As one reaches the base of the sacred hill, one encounters a stone stairway with a hundred steps. This leads up to a large enclosure surrounded by long, narrow buildings with colonnaded porches; these are the living quarters for the cult's priests. Inside the enclosure rests the temple, its front lined with four columns, these being much larger than those supporting the porches. Walking inside the temple,

A statue of Serapis, who brings fertility to the earth's surface. Each year thousands of tourists visit his temple in the city's southwestern sector.

A Therapeutic Dream

As a healing god, Serapis is often identified with the Greek god Asclepius and Egyptian god Imhotep (whom the Greeks call Imouthes). All have been known to visit sick people in dreams; because these visits usually bring about an improvement in health, they are often referred to as therapeutic dreams. This account (quoted in Naphtali Lewis's Greeks in Ptolemaic Egypt) *tells of such a dream:*

I was suddenly seized with a pain in my right side, [and] rushed to the helper of the human race [Serapis/Asclepius/Imhotep]. . . . It was night, when every living creature was asleep except those in pain, and divine influence could manifest itself more effectively. I was burning with a high fever and convulsed with panting and coughing. . . . I was dropping off to sleep . . . but my mother . . . sat by my side without sleeping a wink. Then suddenly . . . there came to her a divine apparition . . . a figure, taller than human, clad in shining raiment [and] carrying a book in his left hand; it only looked at me from head to foot two or three times and disappeared. My mother, after recovering herself . . . found me sweating profusely but free of fever. . . . She started to tell me about the god's potency, but I anticipated her. . . . Everything she had seen in the vision had appeared to me in dreams. . . . Assemble, all who have served the god and been cured of diseases . . . all who have been rescued from dangers at sea. For every place has been visited by the saving power of the god.

the visitor finds a huge statue of the god wrought of wood and metal and beautifully decorated. (All may enter to see this marvel. But keep in mind that no worship takes place inside the temple, so as to respect the god's privacy; sacrifices take place at small altars on the temple's grounds.)

This great cult statue of Serapis is involved in one of the most visually stunning and moving religious events in the Mediterranean world. In the temple's eastern wall, facing the direction of the sunrise, there is a large window. Once each year, on the day most sacred to the god, shafts of sunlight enter the window at just the right angle to illuminate his lips and mouth; the thousands of expectant people gathered outside invariably gasp, realizing that this divine "kiss" of the sun energizes and appeases the god, ensuring that he will continue to look kindly on and protect the community.

Isis's Temple and Festivals

Another important temple that all tourists coming to Alexandria will want to visit is that of the goddess Isis, located not far north of the Soma, where Alexander's tomb rests. For those foreigners who may have limited knowledge of this important deity, she is a very ancient Egyptian goddess seen as a devoted mother figure and patroness of the family unit. Through her relationship with her brother and husband, the fertility god Osiris, she also strongly personifies nature's reproductive forces. In the fourth century B.C., her worship spread to Greece, where she is identified with the agricultural goddess Demeter, also a fertility deity. (Some Greeks also view Isis as a manifestation of the love goddess, Aphrodite.) And in the three centuries that followed, Isis's cult spread across the Mediterranean world, even to Rome.

The rituals and beliefs of Isis's cult, as visitors to her sanctuary in Alexandria learn firsthand, include initiation, baptism, and the promise of eternal salvation. According to the tenets of the faith, the goddess appears to initiates in a dream to signify that she has chosen them to follow her. Initiates take a special bath to purify themselves and fast for ten days. Then Isis's priests allow the new members, along with other worshipers, to enter the temple grounds; there, all view the sacred objects, the nature of which is known only to members.

For those interested in attending daily services at the Alexandrian temple, regular worship takes place four times a day. Just before dawn there is a public ritual on the temple grounds; at noon the sanctuary is open for private prayer and meditation; and two more public services take place in the late afternoon and early evening, after which the temple closes for the night.

Isis sits on an ebony throne in this popular statue of the goddess. Her worship promises eternal salvation.

Isis's Appearance

In his popular novel, The Golden Ass, *the Roman writer Apuleius gives this description of the goddess Isis, which nicely summarizes the common view of her:*

To begin with, she has a full head of hair which hangs down, gradually curling as it spreads loosely and flows gently over her divine neck. Her lofty head is encircled by a garland interwoven with diverse blossoms, at the center of which above her brow is a flat disk resembling a mirror, or rather the orb of the moon, which emits a glittering light. The crown is held in place by coils of rearing snakes . . . and adorned above with waving ears of corn. She wears a multicolored dress woven from fine linen, one part of which shines radiantly white, a second glows yellow with saffron blossom, and a third blazes rosy red. . . . [A] jet-black cloak gleams with a dark sheen as it envelops her. . . . The garment hangs down in layers of successive folds, its lower edge gracefully undulating [rippling] with tasseled fringes.

Visitors should also take note of the dates of Isis's two annual festivals. The Festival of Seeking and Finding will take place between October 28 and November 3. The highlight is a reenactment of the goddess's diligent search for the parts of Osiris's body after his murder and dismemberment. The other festival, the Launching of Isis's Ship, will take place on March 5 to celebrate the advent of spring and the renewal of life that accompanies it. The Roman writer Apuleius's recently published and very popular novel, *The Golden Ass*, contains this excellent description of what visitors can expect:

The chief priest names and consecrates to the goddess a ship which has been built with splendid craftsmanship. . . . Holding a flaming torch, he first pronounces most solemn prayers . . . and then with an egg and sulfur he performs over it an elaborate ceremony of purification. The bright sail of this blessed craft carries upon it woven letters in gold, bearing . . . petitions for trouble-free sailing on its first journeys. . . . Then the entire population, devotees and uninitiated alike, vie in piling the ship high with baskets laden with spices and similar offerings, and they pour on the waves libations [liquid offerings] of meal soaked in milk. Eventually the ship, filled with generous gifts . . . is loosed from its anchor-ropes and launched on the sea before a friendly, specially appointed breeze. Once its progress has caused it to fade from sight, the bearers of sacred objects . . . make their eager way back to the temple.[19]

Other Religious Information of Note

Besides the temples of Serapis and Isis, the most popular religious site in the city is the Paneum, the temple of Pan, the Greek god of shepherds, pastures,

In Isis's March festival, worshipers carry her gift-laden ship to the sea, where they will launch it with great ceremony.

The Fun-Loving but Formidable Pan

It is perhaps fitting that pleasure-loving Alexandrians would embrace one of the most fun-loving of all the gods—Pan, worshiped at one of the city's best-known temples, the Paneum. In Greco-Roman tales of the god, he often lusts after and plays with various nymphs (minor nature goddesses). One of his most famous stories relates how he took part in a music contest with Apollo, god of prophecy. Because Midas, the Greek king who acted as judge, chose Pan the winner, Apollo gave Midas an ass's ears as a punishment.

Believers hold that, though Pan is artistic and fun-loving, he can also be quite serious and formidable, with an especially loud voice said to be frightening at times. For example, Pan's voice struck fear into the hearts of the race of giants that did battle with the Olympian gods at the dawn of time. It is also said that in the Battle of Marathon, in 490 B.C., in which the Greeks won a great victory over the Persians, Pan made the Persians panic and flee the field. In gratitude, the Greeks instituted regular sacrifices to him.

and flocks (whom the Romans identify with their woodland gods Faunus and Silvanus). Artists and writers usually depict Pan with a human upper body and a goat's legs, ears, and horns. He also carries his familiar pipe with seven reeds (the *syrinx*, or "pan-pipes"), said to be his own invention.

The Paneum is located just southeast of the Soma, not far from Isis's sanctuary. Pan's sanctuary rests atop an artificial hill created by the early Ptolemies, equipped with a spiral walkway that winds its way to the summit. From there, the entire city is visible.

CHAPTER SIX

Athletics, Sports, and Games

The vast majority of visitors who arrive in Alexandria each year either attend public athletic competitions and games or seek out places where they can exercise, play sports, and relax. This is not surprising. After all, physical fitness, sports, and games—collectively termed physical culture—are an integral element of societies across the Mediterranean world.

What makes Alexandria's physical culture unique, to the delight of tourists and other visitors, is its cosmopolitan nature. It is the only large city in the known world that combines elements of Egyptian, Greek, and Roman culture, and the sports and games practiced here reflect that unusual and colorful mix. Some of the informal games played by both children and adults on the streets and in the waterways are traditional Egyptian pastimes dating back countless centuries. These coexist with informal Greek games, as well as more formal Greek gymnasia and athletic contests. And the most recent addition—large-scale Roman facilities for gladiatorial fights and chariot races—provide still another outlet for fun and leisure.

Relaxing at the Gym

Whether the visitor claims an Egyptian, Greek, Roman, Gallic, Syrian, Arabic, Persian, or some other birthright, he will want to spend at least part of his stay in Alexandria relaxing. To this end, a Greek gymnasium is highly recommended.[20] The city's main gymnasium is located on the south side of the Canopic Way, across from the athletic stadium and palace sector. A number of smaller gyms can be found in various other parts of the city, although none can accommodate as many people or have as many amenities as the main facility.

On the one hand, such gymnasia feature rooms for changing, exercising, bathing, and socializing. One can work out with weights, for instance. The dumbbells, which strengthen the upper body, are called *halteres*. They are made of lumps of lead or stone molded or carved with recessed areas for gripping with the hands, and they vary in weight. One can also engage in friendly wrestling matches in the section of the gymnasium called the *palaestra*. (For those unfamiliar with Greek language and culture, *palaestrae* were originally separate facilities devoted to wrestling, but the term has also come to denote

Among the more popular Greek-style athletic events are the discus and javelin throws. In this drawing, local athletes prepare for these events as their coach (left) looks on.

any room or area where wrestling matches take place.)

The gymnasium also has an adjacent field for practicing various athletic events and games. These include throwing the discus and javelin. And many people find the long jump particularly challenging, as well as relaxing. For this activity, one holds *halteres* weighing between two and ten pounds. In fact, these weights were originally invented for jumping, as revealed by the fact that the Greek word for jumping is *halma*. According to the Greek writer Philostratus, if one uses the *halteres* properly, "then guidance of the hands is unfailing and brings the feet to the ground without wavering and in good form."[21]

After working up a sweat, patrons can attend a Roman-style bath. Standard are cold and hot pools, as well as a sauna and a massage area. For those who want to unwind further after bathing, the main bathhouse has a small library and some quiet reading rooms. Best of all, the traveler will be happy to learn that all of these amenities are inexpensive; admission to a gym costs only a few obols.

Greek-Style Athletics

The visitor who casually attends the city's gymnasia cannot help but notice a small group of individuals who exercise much more regularly and vigorously. They are training for Greek-style athletic competitions, which are staged both locally and abroad. The local contests take place during certain religious festivals in the stadium located across the Canopic Way from the main gymnasium. Travelers are strongly urged to attend these exciting events. Of the outside competitions, by far the most famous and prestigious, of course, is the Olympic Games, held every four years at the sacred sanctuary of Olympia, in southern Greece. Being Greeks, the Ptolemies eagerly supported training Alexandrian athletes and sending them to the Olympics, and the tradition has remained strong ever since.

The events one will witness in the contests held in the Alexandrian stadium are for the most part the same as those at the Olympics and most other panhellenic ("all-Greek") games. Footraces are standard. They include staples like the *stade*, a sprint of about six hundred feet; the *diaulos*, a two-*stade* run; and the *dolichos*, a longer run of twenty-four *stades*. There is also a *stade* for boys under eighteen. Another important footrace is the race in armor, or *hoplitodromos*. It takes its name from *hoplite*, the Greek term for a heavily armored infantry soldier. Each runner wears a bronze helmet and greaves[22] and carries a bronze shield. The race is two *stades* in length (and therefore equivalent to the *diaulos*).

The local Alexandrian games feature a number of other popular events besides footraces. Among these are the

In this spirited wrestling match between two local competitors, the judge stands close by brandishing his rod, ready to punish a rule-breaker.

combat, or "heavy," sports, including wrestling, boxing, and the *pancratium*. (Non-Greeks should take note that the pankration is a very strenuous combination of boxing and wrestling in which punching, kicking, throwing, pressure locks, and strangling are all allowed. Only biting and eye gouging are forbidden. A match ends only when one fighter surrenders, loses consciousness, or dies.) There is also the pentathlon, a grueling test of overall athletic prowess. It consists of five events—the *stade*, wrestling, the javelin throw, discus throw, and running long jump. Completing the program are the equestrian events—races for both chariots and single horses ridden by jockeys. These take place at the circus (hippodrome) located just beyond the city's eastern wall.

Chariot Racing

The differences between Greek- and Roman-style games can be seen clearly in the case of chariot racing. First, before the Romans came along, Alexandria's hippodrome was like most of those across the Greek world—essentially an open field lined with raised banks of earth, on which the watchers stood. The Romans, who are concerned foremost with the comfort of the spectators, transformed the facility into a stone structure with graduated tiers of seats, a protective wall between the racers and spectators, and awnings to protect many of the spectators from the sun.

Roman chariot races are also longer, more violent, and feature professional drivers who sometimes become world-famous sports figures. Many, if not most, of these drivers begin as slaves and rarely gain true social acceptance in polite society, which looks on entertaining as a degrading profession. Yet, like suc-

cessful gladiators, winning racers are widely admired among the general populace. Both on and off the track, young girls often greet them with swoons and squeals of delight.

The races in which these charioteers take part are staged mostly on holidays and other special occasions (such as the celebration of a military

Two wrestlers grapple. Wrestling is the most popular of the combat sports, which also include boxing and the pankration.

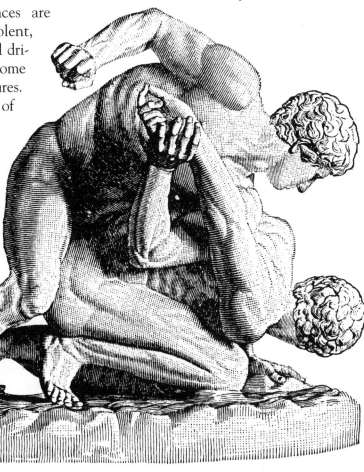

Successful Charioteers Get Rich

Chariot racing can be very lucrative for the drivers, especially winning ones. Although the owners of horses and teams receive the purse money, they pay their drivers, and successful charioteers eventually gain their freedom (if they started out as slaves) and begin receiving hefty percentages of the purse. It is not uncommon, therefore, for popular drivers to become rich men. According to the Roman satirist Juvenal, "You'll find that a hundred lawyers scarcely make more than one successful jockey." One such successful charioteer was Scorpus, who won over 2,000 races and died in a track accident at age twenty-six. Another driver, Calpurnianus, won 1,127 victories, including several that paid him about forty times or more the annual wage of an average Roman soldier. Another popular charioteer, Crescens, began racing at age thirteen and died at age twenty-four, earning well over a million drachmas in his short but glorious career.

victory somewhere in the empire). Usually twelve races are held each day, although on occasion there might be as many as twenty-four. The chariots move around the *euripus* (or *spina*), a stone axis running lengthwise down the middle of the track.

Meanwhile, the crowds that watch these races consist of a mix of men, women, freedmen (freed slaves), and slaves. Admission is free. Visitors who plan to stay for most or all of the races are advised either to bring along a pillow or to rent one from a vendor at the track, as sitting on the stone seats can become rather uncomfortable after a couple of hours. As at other public games facilities, fast food is available from roving vendors, as well as at snack bars located beneath the stands.

The Gladiatorial Combats

The races in the circus sometimes feature spills and crashes, and from time to time drivers are killed, adding to the excitement for many fans. Those who enjoy the thrill of danger and potential death will also not want to miss the gladiatorial bouts, held in the amphitheater (or arena) situated about a mile and a half west of the stadium on the Canopic Way. The government posts the dates and times of these combats, which take place less frequently than chariot races, on walls in the marketplace and other high traffic areas in the city.

The men (and on rare occasions women) who fight in these games are mostly prisoners, slaves, and criminals who train long and hard in special gladiator schools like the one that adjoins the local amphitheater. However, a few gladiators are paid volunteers; they usually get involved because they are having financial difficulties, since the winners can earn generous prize money. Other volunteers are motivated by the physical challenge and appeal of danger, or the prospect of becoming popular idols and sex symbols who can have their pick of pretty young girls.

To increase understanding and appreciation of a gladiatorial show for those who have never before attended one, the following synopsis is provided. First, the gladiators enter the arena in a colorful parade known as the *pompa*. They are usually accompanied by jugglers, acrobats,

Two charioteers are neck and neck as they near the turn and head into the home stretch. No visit to Alexandria would be complete without attending the races.

Origins of Gladiatorial Bouts

The Romans borrowed the idea of gladiatorial combats from an earlier Italian people, the Etruscans, who inhabited Etruria, the region just north of the city of Rome. The Etruscans believed that when an important man died, his spirit required a blood sacrifice to survive in the afterlife. So outside these individuals' tombs they staged rituals in which warriors fought to the death. In Rome the gladiatorial combats were at first private affairs staged by aristocrats. Over time, however, both they and the general populace came to view these games more as entertainment than funeral ritual, and demand grew for making them part of the public games. The renowned general Julius Caesar was the first leader to stage large-scale public bouts. In 65 B.C. he presented 320 pairs of gladiators. This made his political opponents fearful because they worried that he might use these expert warriors against them; so the legislators rushed a bill through the senate that limited the number of gladiators that anyone might keep in Rome.

and other performers, all of whom march to tunes provided by musicians playing trumpets, flutes, drums, and sometimes a large hydraulic organ. (The organ also plays during the actual fighting, heightening the excitement.) Following the *pompa*, the acrobats and other minor performers exit. Then an official inspects the fighters' weapons to make sure they are sound and well sharpened. Finally, the gladiators soberly raise their weapons toward the highest-ranking official present (usually the local governor or the magistrate in charge of the games) and shout, "We who are about to die salute you!"

After that, the first pair fights. The combat can end in several different ways, one being a draw (if both warriors fight bravely and cannot defeat each other); in such a case, the magistrate allows them to leave the arena and fight another day. On the other hand, sometimes both officials and spectators feel the fighters are not giving it their all. Or one man turns and runs. These offenders are punished by whipping or branding with hot irons.

A more common outcome is when one gladiator goes down wounded. He is allowed to raise one finger, a sign of appeal for mercy, after which the magistrate decides his fate, usually in accordance with the crowd's wishes. If the decision is death, he must accept his fate and allow the victor to finish him off. Another possible outcome is when one fighter kills an opponent outright, and still another when the fallen combatant pretends to be dead. No one is successful at this ruse. Men with hot irons run out and apply them to all the bodies, and any fakers exposed in this way promptly have their throats cut.

Popular Informal Games and Activities

For those visitors who prefer more informal games to relax or pass the time, Alexandria has much to offer. One will see ball games of various kinds being played in bathhouses, gyms, private clubs, and in the streets. All types of balls are available, including the *harpastum* (small, hard, and stuffed with hair), the *pila* (medium-sized, and stuffed with feathers), and the *follis* (a large animal bladder filled with air).

One of the more popular ball games played in the city is a team sport, *episkyros*, described here by Greek scholar Julius Pollux:

This [game] is played by [two] teams of equal numbers standing opposite

Among the finest athletes one will find in Alexandria are the acrobats who perform at city-wide festivals, as well as private dinner parties.

Many kinds of gladiators fight in the arena. Amont the most popular is the retiarius, *or net man, who tries to ensnare or trip his opponent with his net and then stab him with his trident, or three-pronged spear.*

one another. They mark out a line between them with stone chips; this is the *skyros* [scrimmage line], on which the ball is placed. They then mark out two other lines, one behind each team [the goal lines]. The team which secures possession of the ball throws it over their opponents, who then try to get hold of the ball and throw it back, until one side pushes the other over the line behind them. The game might be called a Ball Battle.[23]

Simpler and even more widely played is "keep-away," in which one person tries to hold onto a ball while one or more opponents attempt to gain possession of it. Needless to say, the game can be quite rough-and-tumble, depending on how the participants apply themselves. The highly noted Greek doctor, Galen, who recently studied at Alexandria's Museum, describes the game in his *Exercise with a Small Ball*, advocating it as a way to stay in shape:

[The game] is the only one which is so democratic that anyone, no matter how small his income, can take part. You need no nets, no weapons, no

This finely carved relief sculpture shows men in the midst of a ball game. Like Greeks everywhere, Alexandrian Greeks love to play ball.

horses, no hounds—just a single ball, and a small one at that. . . . The capacity . . . to move all the parts of the body equally . . . is something found in no other exercise except that with a small ball. . . . When for example, people face each another, vigorously attempting to prevent each another from taking the space between, the exercise is a very heavy, vigorous one, involving much use of the hold by the neck, and many wrestling holds. . . . The loins and legs are also subject to great strain in this kind of activity; it requires great steadiness on one's feet.[24]

Some other popular informal sports are played in the water. One, "water joust-ing," has been a favorite of native Egyptians for many centuries. Two or more small boats oppose one another, each having a few rowers and one man standing up holding a long stick. As the rowers maneuver their boats, jockeying for position, the stick-men attempt to knock one another into the water.

Simple rowing contests are another popular pastime. In Egypt, these date back to the days of the ancient kings, called pharaohs, who engaged in such contests with their nobles and soldiers. One can still view a carved description of a rowing match staged by the pharaoh Amenophis II, which claims:

His arms were so strong that he was never faint when he grasped the oar

One of the most popular traditional Egyptian games is water jousting, shown in this very old but well-preserved relief sculpture.

and rowed his arrow-swift ship, the best of the crew of two-hundred. Many were faint after a course of half a mile, exhausted and weary of limb and out of shape; but His Majesty still rowed powerfully.[25]

This same scene is reenacted almost daily along the canals and seashores of modern Alexandria; the main differences are that the participants are not kings and nobles, but ordinary people, and they are not all Egyptians, for as it is in other areas, the city's cosmopolitan nature is readily reflected in its wide range of sports and leisure activities.

CHAPTER SEVEN

Sightseeing in Alexandria

Everyone agrees that, outside of Rome and Athens, Alexandria features some of the most imposing, beautiful, and important monuments in the known world. Indeed, Alexandria has enough attractions to keep a visitor busy for several days. They include the Serapeum and other major religious temples, the vast harbors, the canals, the agora, the main gymnasium, the athletic stadium, the circus, the amphitheater, the tomb of Alexander, and the old Ptolemaic palaces (which must be viewed from the outside, since they are not open to the public).

As long and incredible as this list appears, except for the Serapeum it does not include the most famous and often-visited of the city's sights—the Pharos lighthouse, the Museum, the Great Library, and the Caesareum (the sanctuary celebrating the divinity of the Roman emperors). Following are

directions to and descriptions of these four famous sights.

Location and Construction of the Pharos

The Pharos lighthouse is one of the tallest and most awesome structures in the world. It is counted among the seven wonders of the world and by itself it yearly draws thousands of visitors to a city filled with its own share of wonders. Located on the eastern edge of the Pharos Island, the lighthouse can be seen from far out to sea, as well as from villages located many miles inland. For some five centuries it has withstood tides, storms, and earthquakes, and in that time it has been both a boon to sailors and the prototype for all other lighthouses built across the Mediterranean world. As Pliny the Elder states:

Its purpose is to provide a beacon for ships sailing by night, to warn them

The Pharos lighthouse is a striking sight to all travelers as they approach the city. It is one of the tallest and most impressive artificial structures in the world.

of shallows, and to mark the entrance to the harbor. Similar beacons now burn brightly in several places, for example at Ostia [Rome's port] and Ravenna [in northeastern Italy].[26]

One can reach the Pharos by boat. But the most common route taken by tourists is to follow the Street of the Soma northward to the Heptastadion and take the walkway to the island. There the stone path continues for about a mile along the edge of the bay,

finally reaching the base of the lighthouse.

The construction of the Pharos was a time-consuming and difficult task. Ptolemy I Soter began it in 290 B.C., and it remained unfinished when he died five years later. His son, Ptolemy II Philadelphus, finished and dedicated it in 279 B.C. during a ceremony honoring his parents' memory. The architect was Sostratos, a Greek from Cnidus, in Asia Minor. Alexandrian tourist guides tell a charming story about Sostratos's attempt to ensure that posterity would not forget his contribution. Following ancient custom, Ptolemy II forbade the architect from carving his own name on the edifice. Only the name of the king himself was allowed to appear on the foundation stone at the time the lighthouse was dedicated. But the crafty Sostratos was not to be undone. He carved the following message on the stone: "Sostratos of Cnidus, son of Dexiphanes, dedicated this to the Savior Gods, on behalf of

Pictured are some of the terraced gardens making up the Hanging Gardens of Babylon

The Seven Wonders

The seven wonders of the world were originally listed by the Greek writer and traveler Antipater of Sidon about 130 B.C. Besides the Pharos at Alexandria, they include the three great pyramids at Giza, north of the Egyptian city of Memphis, erected thousands of years ago; the Hanging Gardens of Babylon, a series of gardens built on terraces in the royal palace of a Babylonian king in the sixth century B.C.; the gigantic Greek temple at Ephesus, on the Aegean coast of Asia Minor, dedicated to Artemis, goddess of the hunt and protector of animals; the giant statue of the god Zeus that sits in his temple at Olympia, in southern Greece; the Mausoleum at Halicarnassus, near Ephesus, a magnificently decorated tomb built for the ruler Mausolus by his faithful wife, Artemisia; and the Colossus of Rhodes, a giant statue of the sun god, Helios, erected on the Greek island of Rhodes to celebrate its survival after the failed attack and siege by the Greek conqueror Demetrius in 305 B.C. Pottery and bronze models of all of these structures are on sale at shops in the Alexandrian agora.

those who sail the seas."[27] Then he covered the message over with plaster and when it dried carved into it the obligatory words honoring Ptolemy. Low and behold, as the centuries went by, rain and wind wore away the plaster, erasing the king's name and leaving Sostratos's, which is still plainly visible!

Upward Through the Pharos

The Pharos consists of three main sections, one resting atop another. The lowest and most massive section is about 197 feet (60 m), or eighteen stories, in height and square-shaped. One reaches its two outside doors via large staircases, and it contains many dozens of rooms, many of which are used to store the wood and other materials that fuel the fire at the building's pinnacle. Entering the lowest story, one finds a ramp that ascends gradually around the core of the structure, leading visitors to the top of the lowest section. There one finds an observation deck that winds around the base of the building's second section. Guides often stop here and point out the city's most prominent monuments. This allows the visitors to enjoy a needed rest before pressing onward and upward.

A group of local scholars welcome a visiting academic in one of the Museum's several large and ornately decorated courtyards.

Finally, the tour continues into the building's second section, which is octagonal (eight-sided) and stands about 98 feet (30 m) high. It features a winding staircase along the outer walls, which are punctuated by small windows situated at intervals of about ten feet. Reaching the top of this second section, one steps out onto another observation deck with a view even more breathtaking than the one from the summit of the lower section.

Finally comes the third section. It is cylindrical (round) and about 26 feet (8 m) high. At the top is an open area where the fire burns at night to provide a beacon for sailors. A large curved mirror amplifies the fire's light. This area is surrounded by a circle of tall pillars, which support a small cone-shaped roof surmounted by a magnificent statue of the great god Zeus Soter ("Zeus the Savior"). The total height of the structure, from ground level to the top of the statue, is some 344 feet (105 m)! Huge and sturdy, this tremendous monument will undoubtedly stand proudly above Alexandria for untold ages to come.[28]

The Museum— Center of Learning

From the observation decks of the Pharos, one can easily see the next famous Alexandrian sight, the Museum. The latter is located on the north side of the Canopic Way, just south of and adjoining the Ptolemaic palace complex. It is not a place to house paintings or old antiquities. The term Museum is here used to denote a structure dedicated to the Muses, the Greco-Roman goddesses of the arts and literature. Indeed, Ptolemy I constructed the Museum in 300 B.C. as a research facility to promote the study of literature and science, and his son invited the greatest scholars in the known world to live, study, experiment, and lecture there. Not surprisingly, the Museum soon became the world's undisputed center of learning.

The outside of the Museum is graced by a long, impressive colonnade. Inside, there is a large central hall with a high ceiling, a place where scholars gather to confer and share information, as well as eat their meals. Their sleeping quarters are located along corridors leading away from the great hall. Much of the remainder of the facility is roughly divided into four sections, each devoted to the study of a different branch of knowledge— including literature, mathematics, astronomy, and medicine. The Museum also features several lecture halls, a library, a botanical garden, a small zoo, and a theater.

The scholars working at the Museum were for a long time subsidized by the Ptolemies, all of whom had a strong interest in the arts and learning. Later, the city's Roman governors carried on this tradition, and they still pay scholars to live and work in the facility. Both the Ptolemaic and Roman years have witnessed much brilliant

The great medical man Galen long worked as a physician to wounded gladiators at Pergamum, as recalled in this scene. From this work he learned much about human anatomy.

and important scientific work. Euclid, a contemporary of Ptolemy I, compiled all that is known about geometry in his textbook, the *Elements*, which is still used in many schools. Another great mathematician, Archimedes, also studied at the Museum before returning to his native town of Syracuse and masterminding its defense against an army of besieging Romans. Another of the Museum's researchers, the geographer Eratosthenes of Cyrene, calculated the size of the Earth; Hipparchus of Nicea created an immense catalog containing all the stars in the heavens and showed how the face of the Earth can be measured by lines of latitude and longitude; and the physicians Herophilus and Erasistratus made great strides in

understanding the intricate workings of the human body.

Two Great Alexandrian Scholars

The latest and perhaps greatest medical man produced by the Museum is Galen of Pergamum (in Asia Minor), who is recognized by many as the foremost medical practitioner in the empire. A brief synopsis of his life and work illustrates how perceptive and gifted individuals who study at Alexandria's Museum often go on to affect the lives of people across the world.

Galen was born about thirty years ago (A.D. 130). He started as a doctor to gladiators in his native town. But after a period of residence and study at the

Museum, in which he conducted numerous important experiments, his reputation steadily grew. Galen accepted much information from earlier Greek medical researchers (including Hippocrates, the father of medicine, and both Herophilus and Erasistratus); however, Galen's own experiments, including dissections of live dogs, pigs, cows, monkeys, and other animals, allowed him to expand the volume of anatomical knowledge. Other doctors who have heard of his work can use this knowledge to help their own patients, so society as a whole has benefited greatly from Galen's work.

The most famous and influential scholar presently working at the Alexandrian

Museum is the geographer-astronomer Claudius Ptolemy (who is not related to the old ruling family of the same name). He first became famous for his great astronomical work, the *Syntaxis* (*Mathematical Compilation*).[29] A long, complex, and elegantly crafted overview of Greek astronomical ideas dating back to the time of Plato and Aristotle (the fourth

The great geographer Claudius Ptolemy has recently compiled an important eight-volume work that maps the known world.

century B.C.), it is the culmination of the noble science of astronomy. In it, Ptolemy explains how Earth is a large sphere resting unmoving at the center of the heavens. It must be in the center, he reasons, since all bodies and weights fall toward its own center. And it has to be unmoving because if it did move, "it would clearly leave [people, houses, and other smaller objects] behind because of its much greater magnitude. And animals and other weights would be left hanging in the air, and the Earth would very quickly fall out of the heavens."[30] Having established that Earth is an unmoving object resting at the center of all things, Ptolemy goes on to explain in great detail how the heavenly bodies move around it.

Ptolemy's other influential work is his *Guide to Geography*, published only recently. It is divided into eight books, the first of which discusses the principles of applying mathematics to geography and mapmaking and also includes a thumbnail sketch of the length and breadth of the inhabited world. The next six books list the latitude and longitude of some eight thousand geographical locations. And the last book gives estimates for the longest day of the year in various latitudes and longi-

Measuring the Earth

One of the greatest achievements of Greek astronomy (and geography)—the measurement of Earth's circumference—occurred in Alexandria. It was accomplished through a brilliant combination of experiment and deductive reasoning by Eratosthenes of Cyrene (284–192 B.C.), a noted scholar at the Museum who long served as director of the Great Library. One day he read in a papyrus scroll that in the Egyptian town of Syene, located about five hundred miles south of Alexandria, vertical sticks cast no shadows at noon on June 21, the summer solstice. Out of curiosity, Eratosthenes observed a vertical stick in Alexandria on June 21 and saw that the stick clearly cast a shadow. Eratosthenes wondered how this difference in shadows could have come about. His conclusion was that the surface of Earth is curved. He reasoned that the sun is so far away that its rays are parallel when they reach Earth. So sticks standing in different latitudes will cast shadows of different lengths. Eratosthenes calculated that the distance between Alexandria and Syene is about one-fiftieth of the full circumference of Earth. Because he knew the distance between Alexandria and Syene was five hundred miles, he multiplied fifty times five hundred and arrived at a figure of twenty five thousand miles.

This detailed drawing shows Ptolemy I Soter inaugurating the Great Library. He sent messengers across the known world looking for manuscripts to fill its shelves.

tudes. Clearly, Ptolemy, a resident and favorite son of Alexandria, has created a guide that will benefit sailors, merchants, and other travelers from cities far and wide for ages to come.

The Great Library

Adjoining the Museum where the brilliant Ptolemy still works is another Alexandrian marvel—the Great Library. It consists of a long colonnaded hall, with a row of small rooms running down each side. The rooms contain storage bins for more than seven hundred thousands manuscripts, by far the largest collection in the world. Scholars like Ptolemy and Galen first locate the books they need in these storage rooms; then they sit and read them at tables set up in the main hall (although sometimes they take them to lecture halls or their private quarters). Visitors should take note that only the government-sponsored scholars have full access to the books. Visiting scholars must get special permission from the library's director to use the facility, and public borrowing is not allowed.

These scholars consult and discuss the latest books acquired by the library while one of the librarians and his assistants shelve some scrolls.

Like its sister facility, the Museum, the Great Library was the brainchild of Ptolemy I. Its first director was Demetrius Phalereus, a distinguished Athenian scholar who had actually governed Athens from 317 to 307 B.C. Demetrius and Ptolemy desired to make the library second to none. So they sent agents with fat purses to all corners of the known world to buy manuscripts. As a rule, older books were preferred over newer ones, based on the logic that the older ones had undergone less recopying and were therefore likely to be more accurate.

When Ptolemy and his immediate successors could not buy manuscripts, they resorted to more underhanded methods. Dozens of their agents waited on the docks, boarded all arriving ships, and confiscated any books they found. Royal scribes made copies of these books and gave the owners the copies, while the originals were added to the Great Library's collection. The most celebrated case of such trickery occurred when Ptolemy III became determined to acquire the original manuscripts of the works of the great Athenian tragic playwrights, Aeschylus, Sophocles, and Euripides. He borrowed the books from Athens, which demanded he leave a cash deposit to ensure their safe return. The amount is said to have been enormous—fifteen talents or more.[31] Once the books had been copied, Ptolemy sent the copies to Athens and kept the originals, gladly forfeiting the deposit.

This quaint story about the Great Library is undoubtedly true. But there have been false rumors about the place that have caused travelers a certain amount of confusion. The most famous example is a reference made by Plutarch in his biography of Julius Caesar. During the battles that Caesar fought in the city in support of Cleopatra, Plutarch claims:

The enemy dammed up the canals and . . . tried to intercept his communications by sea and he was

One of the two famous obelisks called "Cleopatra's Needles" towers into the sky, The needles stand at the entrance of the Caesareum, completed by Augustus.

forced to deal with this danger by setting fire to the ships in the docks. This was the fire which, starting from the dockyards, destroyed the Great Library.[32]

Based on this passage, a good many tourists have come to Alexandria expecting to see a pile of blackened stones where the library once stood. They are always pleasantly surprised to find the place still quite intact and serving its normal functions. The fact is that Plutarch got it wrong. A fire did indeed ignite and spread while Caesar was fighting Cleopatra's enemies; but the books it burned were new ones still stored in warehouses in the dockyards. The Great Library not only survived, it later received a gift of thousands of books from Pergamum, thanks to the efforts of Caesar's successor, Marcus Antonius; and the emperor Claudius (who reigned from A.D. 41 to 54) built a new wing, making the world's biggest library larger than ever.

The Glorious Caesareum

Though by far the largest, the Great Library is not the only library in the city. A fair-sized collection of books can be found in one of the stoas adjoining the Serapeum. And two small libraries grace the Caesareum, the shrine dedicated to the divinity of the Roman emperors. It is located near the shore on the south side of the eastern harbor, just east of the warehouse sector. One can find it easily, even from a great distance, as it features two tall obelisks that tower over all the nearby structures.

The Caesareum has a fascinating history. The last Ptolemaic ruler, Cleopatra VII, began its construction, intending it to be a shrine honoring her lover, Antonius. But the project remained unfinished when the two committed suicide in 30 B.C. Octavian, who would soon become the emperor Augustus, then entered the picture. He desired to eliminate all statues and other monuments to his rival, Antonius, then existing in Alexandria. In the case of the Caesareum, Octavian completed the sanctuary but made it the center of his own cult in Egypt. He and his successors came to be seen as living gods. And this remains the spot where both locals and visitors pay homage to the emperors on the days designated by the Roman governor.

The sanctuary is certainly impressive enough to be worthy of any emperor. The entrance is marked by the two great obelisks, which have come to be called "Cleopatra's Needles," even though Octavian brought them to Alexandria several years after her death.[33] They were originally carved by the pharaoh Thutmosis III more than fourteen centuries ago at Heliopolis (in the southernmost reaches of the Nile Delta). Moving them was no easy task, as each stands sixty-nine feet (21 m) high and weighs almost two hundred tons.[34] As for the rest of the sanctuary, the Alexandrian writer Philo provides this handy description:

There is elsewhere no sanctuary like that which is called the Caesareum, a temple to Caesar [i.e., the emperor], patron of sailors, situated on a spit of land facing the harbors famed for their excellent moorings, huge and conspicuous, forming an area of vast breadth, embellished with porticoes [roofed walkways], libraries, men's banqueting halls, groves . . . spacious courts, open-air rooms, in short everything which lavish expenditure could produce to beautify it—the whole a hope of safety to the voyager whether going into or out of the harbor.[35]

Like so many other wondrous sights in Alexandria, this glorious shrine to the Caesars is not to be missed.

CHAPTER EIGHT

Trips to Nearby Sights of Interest

Clearly, the number of compelling attractions in Alexandria can easily keep a traveler busy for many weeks. Yet it must not be forgotten that the city lies on the threshold of one of the world's oldest and most fascinating lands. Indeed, Egypt features numerous sights of interest, ranging from magnificent stone temples and statues to the country's ancient capital, Memphis, to those world-famous artificial stone mountains, the pyramids of Giza, to immense, completely flat fields of crops, stretching from horizon to horizon, to the life-giving Nile itself, the world's mightiest river, and its awe-inspiring yearly flood cycle. In fact, the Nile is also the liquid highway that leads travelers to most of the other sights; only a few lie more than a few hours' journey by foot, donkey, or camel from the river.

Towns Like Islands in a Sea

The Nile is one of the world's most popular tourist attractions, as well as the entity that makes life and civilization possible in the otherwise barren wastes of the vast Egyptian deserts. The usual way to reach the river from Alexandria is to take a ferry to the mouth of the Canopic branch and from there travel into the Delta. Numerous small boats can be hired, usually owned and piloted by native Egyptians. The pilot will point out important sights on the riverbanks. Yet, for an extra fee, often quite modest, visitors can hire a professional guide who will go ashore with them, lead them to the various local landmarks, and explain their histories.

One of the first points all the guides make is that the Nile is the world's longest river, although no one knows just how long it is, since its source lies deep in the unexplored interior of the African continent. The Nile flows south to north through the middle of the country and in the Delta fans out into many tributaries that empty into the Mediterranean Sea. Nearly all of Egypt's inhabitants live in the narrow but moist and fertile strips of land that run along the river's banks. Only a few small, green oases can be found in the hundreds of miles of parched desert sands that stretch beyond that fertile ribbon near the Nile.

For this reason, all Egyptians are completely dependent on the river. It provides them with the water they need to drink, cook, bathe, and wash their clothes. In addition, it is the highway on which they sail or row small boats from town to town. Overall, as the famous fifth-century B.C. Greek historian Herodotus memorably put it, Egyptian civilization is the "gift of the river."[36]

Of the many ways the Nile grants this gift, probably the most overtly stunning is the manner in which it gently floods over its banks each year, covering the fields, soaking the earth, and laying down fresh deposits of rich soil. "When the Nile overflows," Herodotus wrote, "the whole [inhabited part of the] country is converted into a sea. And the towns, which alone remain above

water, look like islands."[37] Nowhere else in the known world is there a river that floods in this manner, and the sight of the Nile in full flood is simultaneously uncommon, extraordinary, and majestic. So it is not surprising that people come from all parts of the Roman Empire and

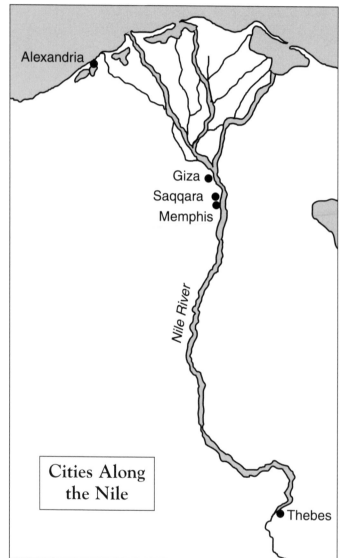

Alexandria

Giza

Saqqara

Memphis

Nile River

Cities Along the Nile

Thebes

The Nile during flood season. Travelers are always impressed by the sight of towns that have been temporarily converted into islands by the gentle waters.

beyond to witness it. Many have tried to describe it in words, including the first-century A.D. Roman playwright and philosopher Lucius Annaeus Seneca (who was so impressed by Egypt that he bought several estates there). "The appearance of the countryside is most beautiful when the Nile has spread itself over the fields,"[38] he wrote.

How the Farmers Live by the Seasons

Thanks to these yearly floods, Egypt produces enormous quantities of grain, more than any other Mediterranean land, as well as many other important crops. From the thousands of square miles of fields along the riverbanks comes the grain that passes through the

A Traveler Gets the Red-Carpet Treatment

Most tourists who travel away from Alexandria and up the Nile must make do with whatever money and personal possessions they can carry. However, wealthy or famous individuals, as well as high public officials, often benefit from special treatment. This letter (quoted in Select Papyri*) was written in 112 B.C. by a palace clerk in Alexandria to an official in Crocodilopolis, a town about sixty miles south of Memphis, to ensure the red-carpet treatment for a visiting notable:*

Lucius Memmius, a Roman senator in a position of considerable importance and honor, is sailing [up the Nile] from Alexandria to . . . see the sights. Receive him in the grand style, and see to it that, at the usual points, lodgings are prepared and landing facilities to them are completed . . . and that the gifts, a list of which is attached below, are presented to him at the landing places. Also provide furniture for lodgings, the special food for feeding to [the local crocodile god] and the crocodiles. . . . In general, remember to do everything possible to please him; put forth all your efforts.

dockyards at Alexandria and then proceeds to the hungry populations of Rome and other Mediterranean cities. River guides will gladly take visitors on side trips to see the workings of local farms and vineyards up close. One will find the natives hardworking, earnest, and exceedingly friendly. It is not unusual for a poor farmer to offer a stranger lunch, or even supper, as well as congenial conversation. (It should be noted that many of the peasants speak neither Greek nor Latin; however, this usually presents no serious barrier, since most of the guides are bilingual and will translate.)

For these peasant farmers, who form the backbone of the country's economy, the Nile's repeated rising and falling provides a way to measure time and the seasons and plan activities. As they themselves explain it, they recognize three seasons. The first is *akhet*, the "inundation," when the river's waters rise and cover the land. This season lasts from July through September. Then comes *peret*, which begins in October when the waters retreat from the land. From then until February, the farmers plant their seeds in soil so soft and rich that it is often unnecessary to plow first! Typically, they spread their seeds on top of the soil and use their plows to turn over the earth and cover them. Some farmers never plow at all, choosing instead to bury the seeds by letting their sheep and pigs trample the soil.

Finally, comes the season of *shemu*, lasting from February to June, when the farmers harvest their crops. Using wooden sickles, lines of reapers march along, cutting down the wheat, barley, or flax (which is used in making clothes). Gangs of women and children follow the reapers and gather up the felled stalks into wicker baskets. To separate the grain from the stalks (a process called threshing), the farmers throw it onto a floor made of hard-beaten earth, where oxen, donkeys, or people trample it. After that, the workers load the harvested crops into wooden or stone silos. Government overseers then decide how much will be distributed to local Egyptians and see to shipping the rest downriver toward Alexandria.

Not long after the silos have been filled up and the grain and other crops distributed, the Nile's waters begin rising again in the onset of *akhet*. During the flood season, most farmers cannot work in their fields, so some of them keep busy at basket making, spinning and weaving, and other crafts. During a time long ago, large numbers of peasants spent this off-season working on the grand building projects of the pharaohs. It was free laborers like these who raised Egypt's massive palaces, temples, and the most impressive monuments of all—the great pyramids.

This wall painting of a peasant couple harvesting wheat can be seen in the tomb of a high Egyptian government official who died an unknown number of centuries ago.

Riding the Rapids

When traveling up the Nile, one will eventually come to the first of several cataracts, points where the ground level changes height, causing the water to flow into rapids of varying states of turbulence. The native Egyptians are quite used to dealing with and even playing in these rapids, as related in this excerpt from the Natural Questions *of the Roman writer Seneca. He calls a cataract a*

remarkable spectacle. There [the water] surges through rocks which are steep and jagged in many places, and unleashes its forces . . . in a violent torrent [that] leaps forward through narrow passages. . . . Finally, it struggles through the obstructions in its way, and then, suddenly losing its support, falls down an enormous depth with a tremendous crash that echoes through the surrounding regions. The people . . . embark on small boats, two to a boat, and one rows while the other bails out water. Then they are violently tossed about in the raging rapids. . . . At length they reach the narrowest channels . . . and, swept along by the whole force of the river, they control the rushing boat by hand and plunge head downward to the great terror of the onlookers. You would believe sorrowfully that by now they were drowned and overwhelmed by such a mass of water, when far from the place where they fell, they shoot out as from a catapult, still sailing, and the subsiding wave does not submerge them, but carries them on to smooth waters.

Wonders of the World

In fact, after one has passed through the rich farmlands of the Delta, the great pyramids are the next point of interest as one heads upriver. The low plateau of Giza, on which these monuments rest, is located only a few miles south of the point where the Nile's main stream begins splitting into its Delta tributaries. The pyramids, which are listed among the seven wonders of the world along with the Alexandrian Pharos, are impossible to miss. Indeed, they are plainly visible for miles in all directions.

Almost everyone who takes the trip up the Nile stops to see them up close, and some of the more hardy and adventurous souls actually climb them!

As the local guides tell it, these huge structures were once the tombs of Egyptian pharaohs. Actually, various pharaohs erected more than ninety pyramids across the landscape over the course of many generations. The three that rise at Giza are simply the biggest and most famous. No one knows exactly when they were built, but the general consensus is that they are at least two thousand years old and perhaps even older.

The largest of the three Giza pyramids, often called the "Great Pyramid," was built by the pharaoh Khufu, whom the Greeks call Cheops. It measures about 756 feet (231 m) at the base of each of its four sides and covers an area of more than thirteen acres. Its original height was 481 feet (146 m), but some of the top stones have fallen away (or perhaps were removed), so it stands a few feet lower than that now. When Herodotus visited Egypt six centuries ago and interviewed some Egyptian priests, they claimed that Khufu's pyramid took twenty years to build. "It is of polished stone blocks," the historian wrote, "beautifully fitted, none of the blocks being less than thirty feet long."[39] Some people estimate that the pyramid required more than 2 million of these blocks in all, each weighing an average of more than two tons.

The task of quarrying these stones, dragging them to the work site, and lifting them into place must have been enormously difficult to say the least.

The three great pyramids of Giza dominate the landscape for miles around. The largest was built to house the body of King Khufu, who lived perhaps two thousand years ago.

tiers or terraces. When the base was complete, the blocks for the first tier above it were lifted from the ground level by contrivances made of short timbers; on this first tier there was another, which raised the blocks a stage higher, then yet another which raised them higher still. Each tier, or story, had its set of levers, or it may be that they used the same one, which, being easy to carry, they shifted up from stage to stage.[40]

Mysterious Passageways

The Great Pyramid is also impressive on the inside, where the pharaoh's body once rested. Of course, as with so many other ancient tombs in Egypt and other lands, the coffin and all valuable grave offerings were long ago stolen by tomb robbers. Still, climbing through the mysterious passageways inside the structure is a unique, if somewhat scary, experience. The traveler is warned not to attempt it without at least one experienced guide to show the way. Also, travelers are advised to carry extra torches, as it is pitch-black inside.

It is also quite easy to get lost inside Khufu's pyramid because it contains many corridors and chambers. Based on the layout and placement of the stones lining the corridors, the architect evidently originally planned on a single, simple burial chamber located just beneath the structure. But when this

An Alexandrian artist recently drew this picture of the Great Pyramid under construction. Scholars agree that it must have taken years to complete.

And many a traveler, gaping at the pyramids in wonder, has asked how the job was accomplished. Herodotus provides the following conjecture, based partly on his interviews with the priests:

The method employed was to build it in steps, or, as some may call them, chamber was only partly finished, someone ordered a change, and the workmen created a room farther up, within the body of the building. They completed the roof of this chamber. But then someone, perhaps the pharaoh himself, changed his mind again.

A few feet above this unfinished chamber they fashioned a sort of grand gallery, a room that slopes upward at an angle toward the center of the structure. This impressive gallery is more than 150 feet long and 28 feet high. Its ceiling is constructed in such a way that courses of stone are stacked, each course slightly overhanging the one below it. At the top, the courses come together, forming an arch.

Following the grand gallery, one finally reaches the chamber where the pharaoh was laid to rest long ago. The room is now empty, of course, thanks to the robbers. But standing in the eerie torchlight, the guide will tell how the tomb once contained thousands of objects, including magnificent clothes, fine jewelry, elaborately decorated furniture, beautifully painted vases and cups, gold and silver statues, wonderfully crafted weapons, a splendid war chariot, a boat to bear the pharaoh to the afterlife, and many other artifacts.

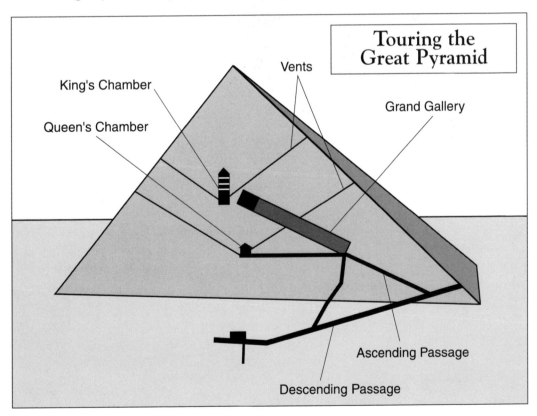

Touring the Great Pyramid

King's Chamber
Queen's Chamber
Vents
Grand Gallery
Ascending Passage
Descending Passage

Memphis and Saqqara

Having marveled at the great pyramids and resumed the trip upriver, in only a few hours one will reach Memphis, the country's old capital. According to legend, at some unknown date in the dim past the first pharaoh, Menes (sometimes called Min or Narmer), united the two Egyptian kingdoms then in existence into one nation. And to commemorate the event he erected Memphis at the former border between the two realms. According to Herodotus, the pharaoh

raised the dam which protects Memphis from the [yearly Nile] floods. The river used to flow along the base on the sandy hills [well west of the city] . . . and this monarch, by damming it up . . . drained the original channel and diverted it to a new one half-way between the two lines of hills. . . . Should the river burst [the dam], Memphis might be completely overwhelmed. On the land which has been drained by the diversion of the river, King Min built the city which is now called

A recent drawing shows the city of Memphis from the east. It was the first capital of Egypt after Menes united the upper and lower kingdoms into a single nation.

The ancient creator god, Ptah, as he appears in a painting on a wall in his Memphis temple.

Memphis . . . and afterwards on the north and west sides of the town excavated a lake, communicating with the river, which itself protects it on the east. In addition to this, the priests told me that he built there the large and very remarkable temple of Hephaestos.[41]

Hephaestos is, of course, a Greek god, whom Herodotus mistakenly identified with the patron deity of Memphis—Ptah, an ancient creator god worshiped in many parts of the country. The god's followers believe that he created the world by a thought coming from his heart[42] and some words uttered by his tongue. Of the numerous temples that rose in the city over the centuries, that of Ptah is the most splendid and most famous. It is a huge stone structure with a roof supported by many tall columns.

In many parts of the temple one can see images of the god painted on the walls. He is almost always portrayed as a mummy wrapped in linen, with his hands protruding from the wrappings, grasping a staff with an ankh sign affixed to the top. (The ankh is a very ancient Egyptian symbol of life.) In these images, the god's head is shaved and covered with a bald cap, and he sports a long black beard.

One of the most popular tourist attractions at the temple is the sacred Apis bull, the herald and mascot of Ptah. The priests in charge of the shrine do not allow visitors to get very close to the sacred animal. But they do allow people to stand at the edge of the temple's inner courtyard and watch the bull take his morning exercise; also, a few privileged individuals are allowed to peek through a tiny window in one of the walls of the stable in which the beast eats and sleeps.

No less popular are the vast necropoli in which the ancient Egyptian royalty and nobility were buried over the course of countless generations. These cemeteries are located to the west and northwest of the city's heart. The biggest and most splendid necropolis is that of Saqqara, which covers an area about 3½ miles (6 km) long. There, one can see numerous pyramids of various sizes. The most famous of the lot is the so-called Step Pyramid of Djoser; among the others dotting the area are those of Sekhemkhet, Userkaf, Teti, and Pepy I. These are all much smaller than the great pyramids at Giza. But some of the Saqqara pyramids are in a remarkable state of preservation and well worth taking the time to see. Saqqara also features hundreds of mastabas—low, flat-topped brick structures used as tombs. (It must be emphasized that all of the tombs at Saqqara, like those at Giza, were long ago looted of all their valuables.)

Farewell to Alexandria

Having seen Memphis and its surrounding region, a few tourists have the time, money, and interest to travel even farther upriver. Many wonders certainly await them, including the temples and palaces of the country's other ancient capital, Thebes, and numerous sacred religious sanctuaries. But the time for such side trips is limited for most travelers, who must leave the venerable antiquities of Memphis and Giza behind and return to the more modern atmosphere of Alexandria.

Regrettably, in time they must bid farewell to that city, too. But they leave with fond memories of wonders that can be seen nowhere else. And they long to return to that special place where East and West meet in a unique blend of architectural and intellectual splendor.

Notes

Chapter 1: A Brief History of Alexandria

1. Homer, *Odyssey*, trans. E.V. Rieu. Baltimore: Penguin Books, 1961, p. 73.
2. Plutarch, *Life of Alexander*, in *The Age of Alexander: Nine Greek Lives by Plutarch*. trans. Ian Scott-Kilvert. New York: Penguin, 1973, pp. 281–82.
3. Plutarch, *Alexander*, in *Age of Alexander*, p. 282.
4. What is now Turkey.
5. Modern writers often refer to him as Mark Antony.
6. Quoted in Theodore Vrettos, *Alexandria: City of the Western Mind*. New York: Free Press, 2001, p. 78.
7. In A.D. 215, some fifty-five years after this guide was allegedly written, the city witnessed its worst anti-Roman riot ever. The reigning emperor, Caracalla, responded by unleashing his troops, who butchered perhaps tens of thousands of Alexandrians.

Chapter 2: Weather and Physical Setting

8. Pliny the Elder, *Natural History*, excerpted in *Pliny the Elder: Natural History: A Selection*, trans. John H. Healy. New York: Penguin Books, 1991, p. 60.
9. Diodorus Siculus, *Library of History*. Various trans. Cambridge, MA: Harvard University Press, 1962–1967, vol. 8, p. 267.
10. The name Heptastadion means "seven stadia in length," referring to the fact that the causeway was seven stadia long. One stade equaled about six hundred modern feet.
11. Julius Caesar, *Commentary on the Civil Wars*, published in *War Commentaries of Caesar*, trans. Rex Warner. New York: New American Library, 1960, pp. 332–33.

Chapter 3—Transportation, Lodging, and Food

12. Quoted in Lionel Casson, *Travel in the Ancient World*. Baltimore: Johns Hopkins University Press, 1994, pp. 161–162. Note that this letter dates from the early fifth century A.D.; however, beliefs about and reactions to such storms were then no different from those in the earlier century in which this guide was allegedly written.
13. Quoted in Casson, *Travel*, p. 204.

Chapter 4: Shopping, Commerce, and Industry

14. The region now encompassed by France and Belgium.
15. Pliny the Elder, *Natural History*, p. 175.
16. Pliny the Elder, *Natural History*, pp. 176–77.
17. The codex was the direct ancestor of the bound books familiar today.

Chapter 5: Temples and Gods

18. Arrian, *Anabasis Alexandri*, published as *The Campaigns of Alexander*, trans. Aubrey de Sélincourt. New York: Penguin Books, 1971, p. 149.
19. Apuleius, *The Golden Ass*, trans. P.G. Walsh. New York: Oxford University Press, 1995, pp. 228–29.

Chapter 6: Athletics, Sports, and Games

20. The word *gymnasium* comes from the Greek term *gymnos*, meaning naked, since Greek athletes often trained and competed in the nude.
21. Quoted in Waldo E. Sweet, ed., *Sport and Recreation in Ancient Greece: A Sourcebook with Translations*. New York: Oxford University Press, 1987, p. 228.
22. Lower-leg protectors, usually made of bronze.
23. Quoted in H.A. Harris, *Sport in Greece and Rome*. Ithaca, NY: Cornell University Press, 1972, p. 86. It is possible that *episkyros* is the dis-

tant ancestor of modern rugby and football.
24. Galen, *Selected Works*, trans. P.N. Singer. New York: Oxford University Press, 1997, pp. 299–300.
25. Quoted in Vera Olivova, *Sport and Games in the Ancient World*. New York: St. Martin's Press, 1984, p. 51.

Chapter 7: Sightseeing in Alexandria

26. Pliny the Elder, *Natural History*, p. 353.
27. This is the version given by the Greek writer Lucian of Samosata. The identity of the "Savior Gods" Sostratos mentions is unclear. He may have meant Ptolemy I Soter and his wife, Berenice; or the twin Greco-Roman deities Castor and Pollux; or Zeus Soter, a manifestation of the leading Greek god, and various sea gods.
28. Compared with most other ancient structures, the Pharos did last a long time—apparently until 1303, when a large earthquake finally destroyed it. In the late fifteenth century, the Turkish sultan of Egypt, Kait Bey, erected a fortress on the same spot, utilizing the stones from the fallen lighthouse. The fortress still stands.
29. Today, it is known as the *Almagest*, the name given to it by medieval Arabic scholars.
30. Ptolemy, *Almagest*, trans. R. Catesby Taliaferro, in *Great Books of the*

Western World, vol. 16. Chicago: Encyclopaedia Britannica, 1952, p. 11.

31. This sum was equivalent to many millions of today's dollars.

32. Plutarch, *Life of Caesar*, in *Fall of the Roman Republic: Six Lives by Plutarch*, trans. Rex Warner. New York: Penguin Books, 1972, p. 291.

33. Actually, this name was not coined until medieval times, when many travelers mistakenly attributed any and all Alexandrian ruins to the famous Egyptian queen.

34. In the late 1800s, one of the obelisks was transported to London and the other to New York. Both still stand and continue to delight tourists.

35. Philo, *Embassy to Gaius*, quoted in Jean-Yves Empereur, *Alexandria Rediscovered*. New York: George Braziller, 1998, pp. 112–13.

Chapter 8: Trips to Nearby Sights of Interest
36. Herodotus, *The Histories*, trans.

Aubrey de Sélincourt. New York: Penguin Books, 1972, p. 131.

37. Herodotus, *Histories*, p. 165.

38. Seneca, *Natural Questions*, trans. Thomas H. Corcoran. Cambridge, MA: Harvard University Press, 1972, vol. 1, p. 77.

39. Herodotus, *Histories*, p. 179.

40. Herodotus, *Histories*, p. 179. Though not implausible, Herodotus's theory does not account for how new stones were carried to the level utilizing the working hoist he describes. Most modern scholars believe that teams of workmen placed the stone blocks on rows of logs, which acted as rollers. To get the blocks up to the pyramid's higher levels, they piled huge earthen ramps around the structure. Then, when the work was finished, they removed the earth, revealing the finished pyramid.

41. Herodotus, *Histories*, pp. 165–166.

42. Most ancient peoples believed that the heart, rather than the brain, was the seat of the mind.

For Further Reading

Lynn Curlee, *The Seven Wonders of the Ancient World*. New York: Atheneum, 2002. A well-written, informative look at these famous ancient monuments, including the Alexandrian lighthouse.

Laura Foreman, *Cleopatra's Palace*. Discovery Books/Random House, 1999. A beautifully illustrated volume exploring recent discoveries of artifacts from the now lost palace of the Ptolemies in Alexandria.

William La Riche, *Alexandria: The Sunken City*. London: Weidenfeld and Nicolson, 1997. Handsome photographs highlight this synopsis of a recent Egyptian-French expedition to recover ancient artifacts from Alexandria's harbor.

Neil Morris, *Atlas of Ancient Egypt*. New York: NTC Contemporary Publishing, 2000. This excellent book about ancient Egypt contains many maps and also several impressive double-page spreads of specific eras and aspects of everyday life. Highly recommended.

Don Nardo, ed., *Cleopatra*. San Diego: Greenhaven Press, 2001. In a series of short essays, noted scholars tell nearly all that is known about this famous queen and her exploits.

———, *Collapse of the Roman Republic*. San Diego: Lucent Books, 1998. Describes the important characters and events of the mid-to-late first-century B.C. Mediterranean world, including Caesar, Octavian, Antony, Cleopatra, and the pivotal role played by Egypt, particularly Alexandria.

———, *Egyptian Mythology*. Berkeley Heights, NJ: Enslow Publishers, 2001. Aimed at intermediate readers, this book retells some of the most famous Egyptian myths, including the story of Osiris's murder by Seth.

———, *Pyramids of Egypt*. New York: Franklin Watts, 2002. Tells when, how, and by whom the pyramids were built, supported by many beautiful pictures. The target audience is grade school readers.

Major Works Consulted

Ancient Sources:

Apuleius, *The Golden Ass*. Trans. P.G. Walsh. New York: Oxford University Press, 1995.

Archimedes, *Works*. Trans. Thomas L. Heath, in *Great Books of the Western World*, vol. 11. Chicago: Encyclopaedia Britannica, 1952.

Arrian, *Anabasis Alexandri*, published as *The Campaigns of Alexander*. Trans. Aubrey de Sélincourt. New York: Penguin Books, 1971.

Kenneth J. Atchity, ed., *The Classical Greek Reader*. New York: Oxford University Press, 1996.

M.M. Austin, ed., *The Hellenistic World from Alexander to the Roman Conquest: A Selection of Ancient Sources in Translation*. Cambridge, UK: Cambridge University Press, 1981.

Julius Caesar, *Commentary on the Civil Wars*, published in *War Commentaries of Caesar*. Trans. Rex Warner. New York: New American Library, 1960.

Morris R. Cohen and I.E. Drabkin, *A Source Book in Greek Science*. Cambridge, MA: Harvard University Press, 1948.

Diodorus Siculus, *Library of History*. 12 vols. Various trans. Cambridge, MA: Harvard University Press, 1962–1967.

C.C. Edgar, trans., *Select Papyri*. Cambridge, MA: Harvard University Press, 1989.

Galen, *On the Natural Faculties*. Trans. Arthur J. Brock, in *Great Books of the Western World*, vol. 10. Chicago: Encyclopaedia Britannica, 1952

———, *Selected Works*. Trans. P.N. Singer. New York: Oxford University Press, 1997.

Herodotus, *The Histories*. Trans. Aubrey de Sélincourt. New York: Penguin Books, 1972.

Homer, *Odyssey*. Trans. E.V. Rieu. Baltimore: Penguin Books, 1961.

Lucian, *Works*. 8 vols. Trans. M.D. Mcleod. Cambridge, MA: Harvard University Press, 1967.

Pliny the Elder, *Natural History*. 10 vols. Trans. H. Rackham. Cambridge, MA: Harvard University Press, 1967; also excerpted in *Pliny the Elder: Natural History: A Selection*. Trans. John H. Healy. New York: Penguin Books, 1991.

Plutarch, *Parallel Lives*, excerpted in *The Age of Alexander: Nine Greek Lives by Plutarch*. Trans. Ian Scott-Kilvert. New York: Penguin, 1973; and excerpted in *Fall of the Roman Republic: Six Lives by Plutarch*. Trans. Rex Warner. New York: Penguin Books, 1972.

J.J. Pollitt, ed. and trans., *The Art of Ancient Greece: Sources and Documents*. New York: Cambridge University Press, 1990.

Ptolemy, *Almagest*. Trans. R. Catesby Taliaferro, in *Great Books of the Western World*, vol. 16. Chicago: Encyclopaedia Britannica, 1952.

Seneca, *Natural Questions*. 2 vols. Trans. Thomas H. Corcoran. Cambridge, MA: Harvard University Press, 1972.

Strabo, *Geography*. 8 vols. Trans. Horace L. Jones. Cambridge, MA: Harvard University Press, 1964.

Waldo E. Sweet, ed., *Sport and Recreation in Ancient Greece: A Sourcebook with Translations*. New York: Oxford University Press, 1987.

Tacitus, *Histories*. Trans. Kenneth Welleseley. New York: Penguin, 1993.

Modern Sources:

L. Sprague de Camp, *Great Cities of the Ancient World*. New York: Barnes and Noble, 1993. An excellent, informative synopsis of major ancient cities, then and now, including Alexandria, Jerusalem, Tyre, Babylon, Syracuse, Rome, Athens, Carthage, and others.

Lionel Casson, *The Ancient Mariners*. New York: Macmillan, 1959. This well-researched and well-written study of trade, shipping, warfare, and other aspects of ancient ships, ports, and seamen is a modern classic and highly recommended for all.

————, *Libraries in the Ancient World*. New Haven: Yale University Press, 2001. Another fine study by Casson, this one explores the great libraries of the ancient Near East (including the famous one in Alexandria), Greece, and Rome.

————, *Travel in the Ancient World*. Baltimore: Johns Hopkins University Press, 1994. A classic of its kind, Casson's study of ancient travelers and their conveyances includes a good deal of information about travel to and from Alexandria. This is fascinating, rewarding reading that brings the ancient world to life.

Peter Clayton and Martin Price, eds., *The Seven Wonders of the Ancient World*. New York: Barnes and Noble, 1993. An excellent overview of ancient writings about and archaeological discoveries related to these monuments, including the Alexandrian Pharos, with numerous helpful drawings.

Walter M. Ellis, *Ptolemy of Egypt*. London: Routledge, 1994. The only major modern study of the founder of the Ptolemaic dynasty is well researched and informative.

Jean-Yves Empereur, *Alexandria Rediscovered*. New York: George Braziller, 1998. A beautifully illustrated volume with many reproductions of old drawings and woodcuts showing the city the way it used to look, along with numerous stunning photos of Alexandria today. The text skillfully traces archaeological efforts to find remnants of the ancient metropolis. Highly recommended.

E.M. Forster, *Alexandria: A History and Guide*. New York: Oxford University Press, 1986. A classic guide book in its own right, this is one of the better modern sources covering both ancient and modern aspects of the city.

P.M. Fraser, *Ptolemaic Alexandria*. 3 vols. Oxford, UK: Clarendon Press, 1972. A huge scholarly source (with a footnote section as large as the text) that examines the ancient city in amazing detail, calling on hundreds of ancient and modern sources. Will appeal mainly to scholars.

Naphtali Lewis, *Greeks in Ptolemaic Egypt*. Oakville, CT: American Society of Papyrologists, 2001. Lewis's classic study of Greco-

Egyptian culture contains numerous references to life and customs in Alexandria.

————, *Life in Egypt Under Roman Rule*. Atlanta: Scholars Press, 1999. Another highly regarded study by Lewis, this one covers life in Alexandria and other Egyptian cities after the Roman takeover in the late first century B.C. Highly recommended for serious students.

Vera Olivova, *Sport and Games in the Ancient World*. New York: St. Martin's Press, 1984. This large, well-written volume begins with useful overviews of how experts think that sport originally evolved and of early athletic practices in the Near East and Egypt. The author then examines Greek sports, beginning with the Bronze Age and Homeric depictions, and concludes with Etruscan games and Roman festivals and games.

Alberto Siliotti, *Egypt: Pocket Guide to Alexandria and the Mediterranean Coast*. Cairo: American University in Cairo Press, 2002. A highly informative guide book to the region of the Nile Delta, including the great city of Alexandria.

Theodore Vrettos, *Alexandria: City of the Western Mind*. New York: Free Press, 2001. This spirited, well-researched volume does an admirable job of covering the broad sweep of the city's history and culture during ancient and medieval times for general readers.

Additional
Works Consulted

H. Idris Bell, *Cults and Creeds in Greco-Roman Egypt.* New York: Biblo and Tannen, 1967.

Elias J. Bickerman, *The Jews in the Greek Age.* Cambridge, MA: Harvard University Press, 1988.

John Boardman et al., *Greece and the Hellenistic World.* New York: Oxford University Press, 1988.

Luciano Canfora, *The Vanished Library: A Wonder of the Ancient World.* Berkeley: University of California Press, 1987.

Peter Connolly, *Greece and Rome at War.* London: Greenhill Books, 1998. Mursi Saad El Din, ed., *Alexandria: The Site and the History.* New York: New York University Press, 1993.

Michael Grant, *From Alexander to Cleopatra: The Hellenistic World.* New York: Charles Scribner's Sons, 1982.

———, *A Guide to the Ancient World.* New York: Barnes and Noble, 1996.

Peter Green, *Alexander of Macedon, 356–323* B.C.: *A Historical Biography.* Berkeley: University of California Press, 1991.

———, *Alexander to Actium: The Historical Evolution of the Hellenistic Age.* University of California Press, 1990.

———, ed., *Hellenistic History and Culture.* Berkeley: University of California Press, 1993.

G.T. Griffith, *Mercenaries of the Hellenistic World.* New York: AMS, 1977.

Erich Gruen, *The Hellenistic World and the Coming of Rome.* Berkeley: University of California Press, 1984.

H.A. Harris, *Sport in Greece and Rome.* Ithaca, NY: Cornell University Press, 1972.

David C. Lindberg, *The Beginnings of Western Science*. Chicago: University of Chicago Press, 1992.

Jack Lindsay, *Cleopatra*. London: Constable, 1970.

Roy M. MacLeod, ed., *The Library of Alexandria: Center of Learning in the Ancient World*. London: I.B. Taurus, 2000.

John Marlowe, *The Golden Age of Alexandria: From Its Foundation by Alexander the Great in 331 B.C. to Its Capture by the Arabs in 642 A.D.* London: Trinity Press, 1971.

Michael B. Poliakoff, *Combat Sports in the Ancient World*. New Haven: Yale University Press, 1987.

Sarah B. Pomeroy, *Women in Hellenistic Egypt: From Alexander to Cleopatra*. New York: Schocken Books, 1989.

Samuel Sandmel, *Philo of Alexandria: An Introduction*. New York: Oxford University Press, 1979.

Chris Scarre, ed., *The Seventy Wonders of the Ancient World: The Great Monuments and How They Were Built*. London: Thames and Hudson, 1999.

Alberto Siliotti, *Egypt: Splendors of Ancient Civilizations*. New York: Thames and Hudson, 1996.

Friedrich Solmsen, *Isis Among the Greeks and Romans*. Cambridge, MA: Harvard University Press, 1979.

Antonia Tripolitis, *Religions of the Hellenistic-Roman Age*. Grand Rapids, MI: William B. Eerdmans, 2002.

Index

Picture Credits

© Paul Almasy/CORBIS, 87
© Araldo de Luca/CORBIS, 39, 40, 47, 55
© Bettman/CORBIS, 45, 62
© Christie's Images/CORBIS, 70
© Gianni Dagli/CORBIS, 64, 72, 95
James Davis/Eye Ubiquitous/CORBIS, 35
Freud Museum, UK/Bridgeman A.L., 49
© Historical Picture Archive/CORBIS, 74
© Jeremy Horner/CORBIS, 83
© David Lees/CORBIS, 71

© Erich Lessing/Art Resource, NY, 42, 89
Library of Congress, 17
Mary Evans Picture Library, 76, 78, 81
North Wind Picture Archives, 10,–11, 14, 15, 26, 32, 33, 35, 37, 40, 52, 59, 62, 64, 65, 67, 69, 70, 91
© Reunion des Musées Nationaux/Art Resource, 19, 43, 51
Stock Montage, Inc., 24, 31, 38, 78, 82, 92, 94
© Roger Wood/CORBIS, 57

About the Author

Historian Don Nardo has written numerous volumes about the ancient world, including *The Age of Pericles, Greek and Roman Sport, Empires of Mesopotamia, Rulers of Ancient Rome*, and studies of Egyptian, Greek, and Roman warfare. He is also the editor of Greenhaven Press's massive *Complete History of Ancient Greece* and literary companions to the works of Homer, Sophocles, and Euripides. Along with his wife, Christine, he resides in Massachusetts.

DATE DUE

Demco, Inc. 38-293